SCHOLASTIC

QUICK 4

FOR

YEAR 6

WRITING

Stress-busting SATs solutions

Techniques for top marks

Practice papers provided

Gillian Howell

CREDITS

Author
Gillian Howell

Editors
Sarah Snashall, Liz Dalby, Nicola Morgan,
Kate Element

Series Designer/Designer
Anna Oliwa

Illustrations
Beverly Curl

Acknowledgements
The publishers gratefully acknowledge permission to reproduce the following copyright material:
Curtis Brown (Aust) Pty Ltd, as Licensor for The Estate of Rowena Farre, for the use of an extract from *Seal Morning* by Rowena Farre © 1957, Rowena Farre (1957, Hutchinson & Co). **Egmont Books Ltd** for the use of an extract from *The Wind Singer* by William Nicholson © 2000, William Nicholson (2000, Egmont UK Ltd, London). **David Higham Associates** for the use of an extract from *Charm School* by Anne Fine © 1999, Anne Fine (1999, Corgi Yearling); for the use of an extract from *The Butty Boy* by Jill Paton Walsh © 1975, Jill Paton Walsh (1975, Macmillan) and for the use of an extract from *Watership Down* by Richard Adams © 1972, Richard Adams (1972, Rex Collings Ltd). **The Maggie Noach Literary Agency** on behalf of the author for the use of extracts from *Secret Heart* by David Almond © 2001, David Almond (2001, Hodder Children's Books) and *Heaven Eyes* by David Almond © 2000, David Almond (2000, Hodder Children's Books). **Oxford University Press** for the use of a letter from *Simone's Letters* by Helena Pielichaty © 1999, Helena Pielichaty (1999, Oxford University Press). **Penguin Group (Australia)** for the use of an extract from *The Power of One* by Bryce Courtenay © 1989, Bryce Courtenay (1989, William Heinemann Australia). **Campbell Perry** for the use of the retelling of the story 'The Nightingale' © 2007, Campbell Perry, previously unpublished. **Rosemary Sandberg Ltd** for the use of an extract from *Hiding Out* by Eliazbeth Laird © 1993, Elizabeth Laird (1993, William Heinemann Ltd). **Usborne Publishing Ltd** for the use of extracts 'Juggling Balls' and 'Make our own balls' from *The Usborne Book of Juggling* by Clive Gifford © 1995, Usborne Publishing Ltd (1995, Usborne Publishing Ltd) and an extract 'First faces' from *Usborne Hotshots – Drawing Cartoons* by Alastair Smith © 1995, Usborne Publishing Ltd (1995, Usborne Publishing).
Every effort has been made to trace copyright holders for the works reproduced in this book, and the publishers apologise for any inadvertent omissions.

Post-it is a registered trademark of 3M.

Text © 2007 Gillian Howell
© 2007 Scholastic Ltd

Designed using Adobe InDesign

Published by Scholastic Ltd
Villiers House
Clarendon Avenue
Leamington Spa
Warwickshire CV32 5PR
www.scholastic.co.uk

Printed by Bell and Bain Ltd.

3 4 5 6 7 8 9   8 9 0 1 2 3 4 5 6

British Library Cataloguing-in-Publication Data
A catalogue record for this book is available from the British Library.

ISBN 978-0439-94512-7

The rights of Gillian Howell to be identified as the author of this work has been asserted by their in accordance with the Copyright, Designs and Patents Act 1988.

Extracts from The National Literacy Strategy © Crown copyright. Reproduced under the terms of HMSO Guidance Note 8.

CONTENTS

INTRODUCTION

Quick Fix for Year 6 Writing is designed to support children and teachers in their preparation for the Year 6 SATs writing tasks.

The activities in this book build on and extend key writing skills across a range of genre and text types.

Each of the twenty-five lessons is accompanied by one or more photocopiable pages to help children plan, make notes and organise their writing.

Key skills which will raise marks in SATs tests are emphasised in each lesson.

The lesson plans are designed to

■ provide children with texts to stimulate their imaginations
■ enable children to learn from examples written by well-known authors
■ build on and extend children's knowledge of writing skills
■ cover key elements that will raise children's marks
■ focus on the trickier aspects of effective writing in the narrative and non-narrative writing tasks.

HOW TO USE THIS BOOK

In order to make the book easy to use, the lessons all follow a similar structure: whole class work, paired talk and writing, independent writing and a plenary session. Extra support is provided for children in the Don't Panic sections.

The lessons will help teachers to stretch children while building on and reinforcing existing knowledge.

Each lesson can stand alone, although they would be better followed sequentially in order to build on previous learning. The lessons can be included as part of a wider literacy programme, and taught at any time of the school year, as they do not focus on specific NLS objectives, but on key aspects that are designed to raise marks in the SATs writing tasks.

The majority of the lessons are accompanied by an exemplar text for children to explore and unpick in order to learn and use the techniques employed by successful authors. For example, how authors use inference to involve readers in a story, encouraging readers to infer characters' feelings and motives, taking account of author viewpoint, creating effective openings, dilemmas and endings, creating believable characters, understanding how purpose and audience affects style and tone.

A number of annotated texts are provided to support teachers and children in shared writing, and can be used as a model technique for children to annotate their own texts.

Details of the key features of language,

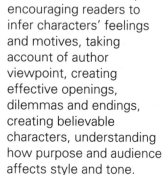

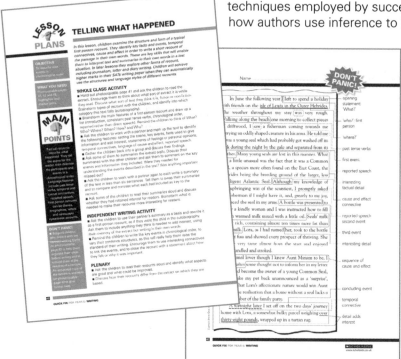

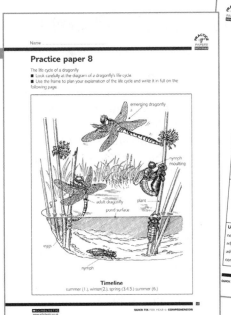

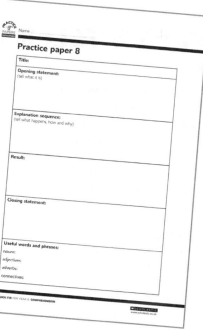

organisation and layout of non-fiction text types are included. These can be used with the whole class, or provided as a checklist for individual pupils to give additional support.

ASSESSING PUPILS'WORK

Ongoing assessment of pupils work should focus on identifying strengths and areas for improvement. This can be formal or informal, using verbal feedback, children's own feedback or written feedback. Children's writing improves when they are clear about what is being assessed before they begin writing. The 'Objective' at the beginning of each lesson plan gives a clear indication of areas for assessment.

Eight sample SATs-style writing tasks are included at the end of the book: four short writing tasks and four long writing tasks.

WHO'S TELLING THIS STORY?

Explain to the children that a story can be told by a first person narrator (using 'I' to describe the events from the narrator's point of view), or by a third person narrator (when the events are reported by someone who does not feature in the story themselves).
When the narration is in the first person, the narrator's point of view and personality can directly affect the way the events in the story are presented, as they can only describe events that their character knows about.

WHOLE CLASS ACTIVITY

■ Hand out individual copies of photocopiable page 7.
■ Explain that it is an extract from a story about three friends who are on holiday and go exploring along the beach together.
■ Tell the children they are going to focus on how the personality of the first person narrator in this extract affects the atmosphere.
■ Ask the children to read the extract to themselves and consider the answers to the following questions: Who are the main characters? Who is telling the story? (Who is the narrator?)
■ Arrange the children in pairs and provide them with writing materials.
■ Ask the pairs to scan the text and collect words and phrases that suggest the character of the narrator. (For example, 'grinned', 'gleefully' – suggesting the character is cheerful.)
■ Next, ask the pairs to draw up a list of words and phrases that describe the other characters in the story. Remind them that all three characters are described from one point of view. Do they think the narrator's opinion of herself and the other characters can be trusted? If not, why?
■ Ask the pairs to annotate a copy of the story extract, marking up first person narration (things that happen to the narrator) and third person narration (things the narrator describes happening to the other characters) in different colours.
■ Ask them to go through the marked-up text with their partner, and discuss the effect of the narrator's voice in influencing how the events are described. Encourage them to consider especially how the narrator uses verbs and adverbs to build a picture of each character.

INDEPENDENT WRITING ACTIVITY

■ Ask pairs of children to choose one of the other characters (Tom or Jess) as narrator, and rewrite the extract (the same events) from their character's point of view.
■ Remind them to think carefully about when to use first and third person verbs, and using the correct tenses.

PLENARY

■ Choose some of the children to read their pieces aloud. Compare and discuss how the stories are similar and different. Point out how the narrator's personality and point of view affects the mood and style of the writing. For example, the character of Tom might change the description inside the cave because he isn't frightened by it; the description on the beach might change when told from Jess's point of view, as she seems excitable.

OBJECTIVE
Manipulate the feel of a piece by changing narrator.

WHAT YOU NEED
Photocopiable page 7, writing materials, different coloured pens or highlighters.

MAIN POINTS

If the narrator is also a character in the story, his or her point of view will affect the way it is told e.g. in a scary story the first-person narrator will show fear; in a heroic adventure the narrator will be brave. It is important to check the verb tenses in a first person narration to ensure consistency.

DON'T PANIC!
■ If the children struggle with how fictional characters' points of view can differ about the same event, illustrate it with a familiar scenario. For example: Two children kick a ball against a wall = fun; Elderly person indoors annoyed by banging = not fun. They will describe the event in a completely different way.

QUICK FIX FOR YEAR 6: WRITING

Sea Cave

Tom and I wandered aimlessly along, kicking at the sand or stopping to pick up the odd shell, while Jess ran from the waves as they rushed in, and followed as they rushed back out again. She kept shrieking when they came too close and running backwards up the sand.

"Jess!" Tom grumbled, "Grow up, for goodness sake!"

Jess shrieked again and carried on.

"I'm bored," he muttered again, as the three of us made our way along the shore towards the rocks and cliffs at the edge of the cove.

"Look Tom," I shouted gleefully. "Jess! Come on. We're going to explore the cliffs."

I ran off with Tom following and Jess left the waves, running to catch us up. We scrambled over the wet rocks, and there, just behind them at the base of the cliff was a dark gap.

"Wow! It's a cave!" I cried, and scrambled my way towards the entrance, slipping and stumbling over the rocks and slimy seaweed. Tom and Jess followed more cautiously.

"Don't go in, Rosie," said Tom.

"Oh, don't be a wimp! I thought you were bored. Come on Jess." Jess scrambled to the entrance with me.

"It looks very dark in there," she said in a small voice.

"It's a Smugglers' cave." I grinned. "We might find some treasure. I'm going in."

I turned as Tom's hand grabbed my arm.

"We were told to stay together," he said pompously. "I'm the oldest. I'll go first."

Tom jumped off the rocks onto wet pebbles while I followed, holding onto Jess's hand. Inside the cave, the floor scrunched noisily as we made our way carefully into the gloomy, dank darkness. It smelled damp and fishy. I began to wish we had stayed in the sunshine outside. The further in we went, the tighter I held onto Jess. The walls were looming over, threatening, and I wanted out.

Suddenly I bumped right into Tom's back.

"What…?" I began.

"Hush!" he whispered urgently. "What's that?"

"What? What's what?" stammered Jess.

"That noise! Listen!"

We stood silently for a moment, eyes wide, trying to see through the dark. Jess gripped my hand tightly. Drops echoed as water made slow sculptures far in the depths. We jumped as the sound of the waves crashed on the rocks outside.

"Got you!" Tom laughed. "Come on," he grinned, turning back towards the light. "We'd better go."

"Yes Rosie, I want to go," added Jess.

I didn't argue. We scrunched back again towards the entrance. As we got nearer, it grew lighter and noisier. The waves sounded louder than before.

"The tide!" cried Tom. "We're trapped!"

SHOWING NOT TELLING

A good writer doesn't tell the reader everything at once, but gives them clues that will make them want to find out more. Readers interpret the clues and make assumptions about characters and outcomes and then are amazed to discover they were right or wrong later in the story. The children will see that using inference in their story-writing will involve the reader and make them want to read on. It will also help them get better marks in their SATs writing paper.

OBJECTIVE
Learn techniques for giving the reader clues.

WHAT YOU NEED
Photocopiable pages 7 and 9.

WHOLE CLASS ACTIVITY
■ Hand out photocopiable page 7 to pairs of children. Ask them to read the story from when the children go inside the cave onwards.
■ While they are reading, ask them to think about how each of the children is feeling and to find evidence in the extract for their opinions. The pairs should discuss their findings, and underline words and phrases in the extract that show how the children feel.
■ Discuss their responses as a class, focusing on one child in the story at a time.
■ Demonstrate how the writer has given an impression that Jess and Rosie feel frightened by what they say and how they say it, rather than telling the reader directly, "She was frightened" or "I was frightened":
  "It's very dark in there," she said in a <u>small voice</u>.
  The further we went, the tighter I held onto Jess. The walls were looming over, threatening, and I wanted out.
  Jess <u>gripped</u> my hand <u>tightly</u>.
■ Demonstrate how the writer shows that Tom is not afraid by describing what he does (for example, he plays a trick to frighten the others):
  "Got you!" Tom <u>laughed</u>. "Come on," <u>he grinned</u>, turning back towards the light.
■ Ask them to look at the last paragraph again, and say if they think the children are trapped, or if Tom is still playing tricks. Children might answer that they are trapped, because the sound of the waves has become louder, or they might think Tom is still playing tricks as implied by the previous trick. In fact, we don't know for sure at this point.

INDEPENDENT WRITING ACTIVITY
■ Hand out photocopiable page 9 to each child.
■ First, ask the children to complete section A of the photocopiable sheet.
■ Next, ask them to discuss each sentence in section B with a partner, and brainstorm what they would do in each situation; what happens when they feel the emotions; how their faces change, what happens inside them. Ask them to picture each situation in their heads and then re-write the sentences in section B to show, not tell, the character's feelings.
■ Finally, ask the children to choose an emotion from the list in section A, and write a paragraph to describe it without using the actual word. They should then swap with their partner and try to guess which emotion is being described.

PLENARY
■ Choose some of the children to read their sentences and paragraphs aloud. Ask the children to choose which ones give them the most vivid picture in their head. Discuss which words and phrases are effective at showing, not telling.
■ Draw up a list of words used that give clues to the character's feelings (for example, verbs and adverbs describing speech and actions).

Sometimes it is more effective to show how your character feels, rather that telling the reader directly. The choice of verbs, adjectives and adverbs can give clues to how characters feel.

DON'T PANIC!
■ Tell the children to picture the scene and how they feel in their head. Ask them to describe how the feeling affects them.

Name _____

Show how they feel

A

Write the word that best describes how each character is feeling next to the sentence. Underline the words in the sentences that led to your decision.

nervous	calm	sad	angry	happy	frightened

1. stamped out of the kitchen, slammed the door and stormed off.

2. With heart beating loudly, she stood, trembling, before the door.

3. During that day, I found myself humming little tunes; grinning suddenly, and hugging myself.

4. "Don't go in!" he begged, gripping my arm.

5. We sat and watched, hardly moving; the warm sun and droning of bees making our eyelids heavy.

6. He watched them turn the corner, and his heart grew heavy.

B

Re-write the sentences to show, rather than tell, the feeling. The first one has been done as an example.

1. He felt angry and he put the book on the table

"He slammed the book down on the table."

2. She heard the dog growling and was frightened as she ran away.

_____

3. He felt happy and excited as he opened the birthday present.

_____

4. When I saw the broken doll, I was sad.

_____

5. He scored the winning goal, and everyone was happy.

_____

6. She sat down, feeling very tired.

_____

www.scholastic.co.uk

PARAGRAPHS AND PUNCTUATION

When we read stories written by good authors, we can learn the techniques they use and use them ourselves, in our own 'voice' or style of writing. The layout of paragraphs and the punctuation of sentences in the text extract for this session help to give the reader a great deal of information in a brief manner. Remind the children how a first person narrator's feelings affect the writing.

WHOLE CLASS ACTIVITY

■ Hand out copies of photocopiable page 11 to pairs of children. Ask the pairs to read the text. Encourage them to look for clues about the setting and characters. Ask them to share their opinions, focusing on one paragraph at a time.

■ For example, the first paragraph simply describes a happy time of being cuddled and sung to. A first-person narrator with golden curls is contrasted with the black nanny; the setting is hinted at by mentioning a warrior, lions and baboons.

■ The second paragraph tells of a disastrous event in just two sentences. The tone is very different from the first paragraph. The verb 'torn' shows what an upheaval this was. The fact that the narrator had a nanny and was sent to boarding school suggests that he was from a wealthy family. Mother and Grandfather are mentioned, but no father. Ask the children what this suggests about the family.

■ The third paragraph shows a new situation by describing a list of specific things. They don't describe the experience; merely suggest it.

■ Ask them to focus on the punctuation in the paragraph beginning 'My Zulu nanny...'. Long sentences are used. What effect do the children think this has? (A sentimental, anecdotal tone, focussing on lovingly remembered details.)

■ Now ask them to compare this with the last paragraph. Ask how many sentences are in this paragraph. (One.) Explain that the sentence is in the form of a list. Explain that semi-colons have been used to separate the phrases in the list. Ask what effect the structure of this paragraph has. (Brisk, detached tone, perhaps suggesting the narrator's wish to forget this part of his life. The expression 'beds that wet themselves' further distances the narrator from the events.)

■ Tell the children that the use of varied punctuation can raise the standard of their own writing.

INDEPENDENT WRITING ACTIVITY

■ Ask the children in pairs to discuss their own feelings on experiencing a major change, such as starting a new school or club, or moving to a new house/town, and to make brief notes.

■ Tell them to use their notes as a basis to write a story opening in two paragraphs, using the structure of the extract as a model. The first paragraph should be about life before the event; the second should describe new feelings or experiences. Ask them to have a go at using the author's technique and write their feelings/experiences as a list.

■ Remind them to show, not tell, their feelings to the reader.

PLENARY

■ Choose some of the children to read their paragraphs aloud.

■ The class should discuss their responses to the story-openings. Do they 'tell' them about how the character felt, or give them clues? Did they make the author's technique work for their own writing?

MAIN POINTS
One way to improve our writing is to try out effective techniques used by other authors. A new paragraph signals new information, for example, a change in person, place or time.

DON'T PANIC!
■ Remind the children that when they change place, person or time, to change paragraph.

The Power of One

1939: Northern Transvaal, South Africa

This is what happened.

My Zulu nanny was a person made for laughter, warmth and softness and before my life started properly she would clasp me to her breasts and stroke my golden curls with a hand so large it seemed to contain my whole head. My hurts were soothed with a song about a brave young warrior hunting a lion and a women's song about doing the washing down on the rock beside the river where, at sunset, the baboons would come out of the hills to drink.

My life proper started at the age of five when my mother had a nervous breakdown. I was torn from my black nanny with her big white smile and taken from my grandfather's farm and sent to boarding school.

Then began a time of yellow wedges of pumpkin burned black and bitter at the edges; mashed potato with glassy lumps; meat aproned with gristle in grey gravy; diced carrots; warm, wet, flatulent cabbage; beds that wet themselves in the morning; and an entirely new sensation called loneliness.

Text © PBryce Courtnay

STAR CHARACTERS

This lesson is about getting to know a character in advance so he or she can be written about with confidence in the SATs writing paper. If the children prepare the details of a character beforehand, and use it in their own writing, they will become familiar with it, as if it were a real person. Then their writing in the SATs writing paper will be easier, the character more realistic and higher marks will result.

WHOLE CLASS ACTIVITY
■ Ask the children which characters they remember from stories they have read recently, and why they remember them. Discuss which characters seem most realistic. What details have authors included that give this effect? What do the children like or dislike about them?
■ Explain that writers get to know their characters really well, as if they are real people. Tell the children that when they write stories, the characters they write about can be any type of person they want, and can look, think and behave however they want. As a writer, they have control over their characters.
■ Explain that if they get to know some characters in advance, and have favourite ones they like writing about, then writing about their character in a test will be quicker and easier.
■ Tell the children they are going to create a character and get to know him or her really well by interviewing him or her as if they were writing a magazine article.
■ Ask the children to work with a partner and take turns to be 'interviewed' as themselves. One child should interview the other for a children's magazine by asking 20 questions.
■ Tell them not to think too long about the questions or answers but to say the first thing they think of. When they have both finished they should discuss how much they found out about each other.

INDEPENDENT WRITING ACTIVITY
■ Hand out photocopiable page 13 to each child.
■ Ask the children to decide on a main character for an adventure story. Explain that the character can be whoever they want, old or young, male or female, good or bad. They should think of a name for their character.
■ Ask them to invent answers to all the questions on the sheet as if the character were being interviewed. Encourage them to add as much detail as they can to make their character seem real.
■ Tell the children to use their answers to write a short paragraph describing the character. Give them five minutes to do this.

PLENARY
■ Ask some of the children to read their character sketches to the others. Discuss how much detail they have included. Are the characters believable?
■ Talk about how a character sketch describes a character in a very direct manner. Remind the children of the work they have done on using inference. Discuss how they could use the details of their characters in a story without telling readers directly. Give them an example: 'Favourite food is pasta' could be written 'He usually rushed home on Fridays; it was pasta night, but this time...'

Get to know your character

Write down your character's answers to the following questions.
Use another sheet of paper if you need to.

Name of character:

1. What makes you feel gloomy or down-in-the-dumps?

2. What sort of place do you live in?

3. Have you got any brothers or sisters?

4. If the answer is yes, do you get on with them? Why?

5. Which clothes do you like wearing?

6. What is your favourite food?

7. Have you got a favourite book?

8. What is your favourite TV programme?

9. What do your friends like most about you?

10. What is your favourite colour?

11. What do you enjoy most when you go on holiday?

12. When and where were you born?

13. Who would you most like to meet?

14. If you were not the shape you are now, what sort of shape
would you like to have?

15. Who is your best friend and why?

16. Do you prefer cities or countryside? Why?

17. What did you dislike about going to school?

18. How do you make your friends laugh?

19. If you had to tell a lie, how would it make you feel?

20. If you could change anything about yourself, what would it be?

Now add a few questions of your own.

TAKE YOUR IDEA FOR A WALK

This lesson introduces the idea of re-using references from earlier paragraphs later in a story in order to give it cohesion. The sample text is from The Water Babies by Charles Kingsley, where three characters feature, are introduced briefly and expanded upon in a later paragraph. The story is written in the third person, so opportunities are available for comparing the different style with the previous first person extracts.

WHOLE CLASS ACTIVITY

■ Hand out photocopiable page 15 to pairs of children. Ask the children to read the extract.

■ Ask the pairs to summarise what each of the three paragraphs is about. Point out how each paragraph introduces new information.

■ Next, ask them to look at how the author has given us details about the characters. First, ask them to focus on the groom. Point out that the groom is introduced in the first paragraph and described only briefly.

■ Ask them to find the groom in the second paragraph and read his description. Does their opinion of the groom change after reading the second paragraph?

■ Next they should focus on the brief description of Mr Grimes in the first paragraph. Ask them to scan the rest of the text and discuss what else they are told about him and where. What impression are they given about Grimes in the last paragraph? Does the author tell them what Mr Grimes' character is, or does he use inference?

■ Point out how the author has introduced the characters briefly at first, and then added detail in later paragraphs. What effect does this have? (It helps to link the paragraphs.)

■ Ask them to focus on the half-brick in the first paragraph, then to find where else it features in the extract. Point out how the author has introduced an idea (the half-brick Tom thinks of throwing) and revisited it later to give cohesion to the paragraphs. Although each new paragraph introduces a new idea or new information, they are linked by references to someone or something that has occurred before. What impression of Tom does the incident with the half-brick give them?

INDEPENDENT WRITING ACTIVITY

■ Tell the children they are going to write three new paragraphs to continue the story and include the following features:

■ Paragraph 1: Preparing to go to Harthover Place by horse and cart the next morning. The horse will kick Tom.

■ Paragraph 2: Travelling to Harthover Place.

■ Paragraph 3: Arriving at Harthover Place.

■ Ask them to take the idea of 'The horse kicks Tom' into the second and third paragraph and to take the character of the groom from the first extract into the third paragraph.

■ Remind them about their impressions of Tom's character and to try to use this in their new paragraphs.

PLENARY

■ Ask several children to read the original text and then their new paragraphs aloud. Discuss which ones work well and why. For example, did they give brief detail in the first paragraph and expand it in later references? Did they retain Tom's personality to give cohesion between the original extract and their new episode?

Name _____

The Water Babies

One day a smart little groom rode into the court where Tom lived. Tom was just hiding behind a wall, to heave half a brick at his horse's legs, as is the custom of that country when they welcome strangers; but the groom saw him and halloed to him to know where Mr. Grimes, the chimney-sweep lived. Now, Mr. Grimes was Tom's own master, and Tom was a good man of business, and always civil to customers, so he put the half-brick down quietly behind the wall, and proceeded to take orders.

Mr Grimes was to come up next morning to Sir John Harthover's, at the Place, for his old chimney-sweep was gone to prison, and the chimneys wanted sweeping. And so he rode away, not giving Tom time to ask what the sweep had gone to prison for, which was a matter of interest to Tom, as he had been in prison once or twice himself. Moreover, the groom looked so very neat and clean, with his drab gaiters, drab breeches, drab jacket, snow-white tie with a smart pin in it, and clean, round, ruddy face, that Tom was offended and disgusted at his appearance, and considered him a stuck-up fellow, who gave himself airs because he wore smart clothes, and other people paid for them; and went behind the wall to fetch the half-brick after all: but he did not, remembering that he had come in the way of business, and was, as it were, under a flag of truce.

His master was so delighted at his new customer that he knocked Tom down out of hand, and drank more beer that night than he usually did in two, in order to be sure of getting up in time next morning; for the more a man's head aches when he wakes, the more glad he is to turn out, and have a breath of fresh air.

by Charles Kingsley

QUICK FIX FOR YEAR 6: **WRITING**

WHO? WHAT? WHERE?

Identifying the key points of Who? What? Where? will help children plan their own outlines before writing a story. This session looks at identifying the key points of an extract and re-using them in a new version. Children are also encouraged to use what they have learned so far: to link their paragraphs, to be aware of narrative viewpoint, and to show not tell.

OBJECTIVE
To identify and use the main points and characters in a story to plan and write a new version.

WHAT YOU NEED
Photocopiable pages 15 and 17.

MAIN POINTS

Establishing who, what and where gives a basic structure on which to work. Modern details such as clothes, speech and background sounds (for example, traffic) can be added to move the setting to modern times.

DON'T PANIC!
■ If children need extra help to structure their paragraphs, give them the following headings:
■ Paragraph 1: Where is Tom? Who else arrives and how?
■ Paragraph 2: Describe the new character's appearance.
■ Paragraph 3: What is important about the new character's visit?

WHOLE CLASS ACTIVITY
■ Hand out copies of photocopiable page 15. Ask the children to re-read the text in pairs and picture the scene in their heads. Explain that they are going to re-write the passage in a modern setting.
■ Discuss the key ideas and main points of the extract. Remind the children about answering literal questions in their comprehension lessons (and looking for Who? What? Where? key points). Discuss what the extract tells them, directly, about the main characters, the setting and the events and write these topics on the board (for example: arrival of the groom, Tom and his master Mr Grimes, Harthover Hall, the need for a chimney sweep).
■ Remind the children what they inferred about the characters (for example, Tom is scruffy as he was offended by the groom's spotless appearance).
■ Ask the children to imagine a similar situation for a modern child. Tell them to take a few minutes and picture it in their heads.
■ Write some of their suggestions on the board and use one of them as a shared writing activity. Ask: How would the appearance of the characters be different? What physical elements would be different? Draw up a list of the children's suggestions.
■ Ask the children to discuss the setting with a partner. Could it be changed while still retaining the basic events? Ask the pairs to underline vocabulary that would not fit into a modern story, and draw up a list of alternative vocabulary (for example: 'the custom of that country' (what usually happened); 'fellow' (man) and so on). Discuss their findings and add them to the board.
■ Now tell the pairs of children to imagine themselves as the main character. What would they see now that is different from Tom's world? What words would they use? Add their suggestions to the details on the board.
■ Discuss what the children inferred about the character of Tom. How could they show this in a modern setting? Model how to include these elements in the shared writing on the board.

INDEPENDENT WRITING ACTIVITY
■ Hand out copies of photocopiable page 17. Ask the children to complete the chart, then to use it to write their modern version of the extract.

PLENARY
■ Choose some of the children to read their pieces aloud.
■ Identify versions that have kept the character of Tom and discuss how this has been achieved.
■ Discuss the modern vocabulary the children have used that gives the same impression as Charles Kingsley's story. Identify details that make the setting relevant to today.

Re-writing in a modern setting

The Water Babies		
Characters (who)	**Character descriptions**	
Tom	■ young ■ cheeky, boisterous	■ works for Mr Grimes ■ been sent to prison once or twice
The groom	■ smartly dressed, clean, round ruddy face ■ riding horse	■ delivering a message ■ works for Sir John Harthover
Mr Grimes	■ chimney sweep ■ cruel and rough	■ gets drunk
Sir John Harthover	■ rich	
Setting (where)	**Setting descriptions**	
courtyard of Mr Grime's home	little detail – outside courtyard, a wall, bricks lying about, big enough for a horse to ride into	
Events (what)		
Groom delivers message to Tom. Sir John needs chimneys swept. Tom wants to throw a brick at him, offended (jealous) of the groom's fine appearance, but he doesn't as groom is bringing work. Grimes hits Tom and gets drunk.		

Modern version	
Characters (who)	**Character descriptions**
1	
2	
3	
4	
Setting (where)	**Setting descriptions**
Events (what)	

17

PLANS

HOW DO YOU SAY IT?

This session focuses on using verbs in reporting clauses to show how a character speaks, as an alternative to using 'said'. This can help children use inference in their writing, as how a character speaks can give insight into their emotions and personality. Using imaginative, powerful verbs for dialogue can quickly result in higher marks.

OBJECTIVE
To use more interesting words as an alternative to 'said'.

WHAT YOU NEED
Photocopiable page 19.

There are many powerful verbs to describe dialogue. Using a variety of verbs to describe speech will give life to their characters and result in higher marks.

DON'T PANIC!
■ If the children get stuck, ask them to speak the words aloud as they want their speaker to say them, and think what they are doing (for example, 'I am shouting', 'I am gasping'). Ask them to imagine the words being spoken.
■ Point out that sometimes 'said' is the right word to use. Tell the children not to overuse powerful verbs.

WHOLE CLASS ACTIVITY
■ Tell the children that in this session you are going to look at ways of describing conversation between characters to make writing more interesting and vivid.
■ Write a brief passage of dialogue on the board, repeating the verb phrases 'she said' 'he said' (for example, "Please tidy your room," she said. "Can't I do it later? I'm busy," he said. "Do it now!" she said.) Ask one or two volunteers to read the dialogue aloud using expressive tones.
■ Discuss how the way you have written it does nothing to help readers get information about the situation or the characters.
■ Explain that the verb phrase, or reporting clause, 'he said' is frequently used to close a character's spoken words. This tells readers what was spoken, but not how.
■ Now write one sentence of conversation on the board three times using 'he said' as the reporting clause, and add an adverb or phrase to show how it is spoken (for example, "Wait for me," he said angrily. "Wait for me," he said in a shocked voice. "Wait for me," he said sadly.) To demonstrate the effect of these qualifiers, ask three children to read only the spoken words aloud and omit the reporting clause, using an appropriate tone of voice.
■ Explain that, to show the children the tone of the speech, you described how the words are spoken, but suggest it could be even better by choosing a more powerful verb to replace 'said'.
■ Ask the children to suggest alternative verbs for 'said' that deliver the same meaning to readers (for example, "Wait for me," he shouted. "Wait for me," he gasped. "Wait for me," he sobbed.)
■ Ask them to work with a partner and draw up a list of as many alternative verbs for 'said' as they can.

INDEPENDENT WRITING ACTIVITY
■ Give the children copies of photocopiable page 19. Explain that the left-hand column describes an emotion. Ask the children to re-write the sentences from the middle column using an alternative verb to show the emotion.
■ Ask the children to revisit their previous writing to see if the dialogue can be improved by changing the word 'said'.

PLENARY
■ Ask the children to take turns to read one of their new sentences aloud. Ask the others to suggest how they think the speaker is feeling, based on the choice of verb.
■ Tell the children to capture some of their favourite words for 'said' in a list that they can remember.

Name _____

Powerful speech

How the character is feeling	What the character says	Alternative verb for 'said'
very angry	'Stop it! You are hurting me,' he said.	
hurt and upset	'Stop it! You are hurting me,' he said.	
frightened	'I can see a huge dog,' she said.	
amazed	'I can see a huge dog,' she said.	
shy	'I'd like to come, too,' he said.	
annoyed	'I'd like to come, too,' he said.	
embarrassed	'It wasn't my fault,' he said.	
pleased	'It wasn't my fault,' he said.	
tired	'It's time we went home,' she said.	
reluctant	'It's time we went home,' she said.	

QUICK FIX FOR YEAR 6: WRITING

GRABBING ATTENTION

The session introduces the idea of 'hooking' a reader with a powerful story opening to make them want to read on. The children explore and practise four different approaches, while re-using the characters they invented in 'Star characters' on pages 12-13.

they invented in 'Star characters' on pages 12-13.

OBJECTIVE
To be able to write a good story opening.

WHAT YOU NEED
Photocopiable page 21, a selection of story books from the class book shelves or library, card or Post-it notes.

MAIN POINTS

The opening of a story can make readers want to continue, or make them give up. Practising four ways to open the story, all with the same character, helps build confidence through familiarity.

DON'T PANIC!
■ Tell children who need extra help to re-use the opening lines from the extracts, but to use their own 'star' character, and add another sentence.

WHOLE CLASS ACTIVITY
■ Discuss any stories the children are reading in their spare time. Ask the children to explain why they are reading these books, and what influenced their choice. If any children answer that the first few lines were good, focus on that point and ask them what it was that particularly appealed to them in the story opening.

■ Explain that the readers often make a judgement about a book or story in the first few lines, so it is important to get their attention. You need a hook to snag them!

■ Tell the children that in this session you are going to look at ways to begin a story that will make the reader want to carry on reading and grab their attention.

■ When they are familiar with a few strong ways of opening stories, they will find it easier to get started when writing in a limited time.

■ Explain that you are going to focus on just four ways of beginning a story. Write four 'hooks' on the board: scene, character, speech and action.

■ Suggest phrases to make the hooks more memorable and write these beneath each hook: Picture This! Who's that? Listen up! Just do it!

■ Explain that photocopiable page 21 has the opening of four different stories by well-known authors. Ask the children to work in pairs and to read the four different story openings. Ask them to discuss what each opening tells them about the story and what sort of story it will be (for exaple, exciting, funny, contemporary, set in the past or the future and so on). Tell them to discuss how each author has grabbed the reader's attention and choose which of the four categories of opening it fits.

■ Next, write the four memorable hooks onto card or Post-it Notes. Place them on different tables. Provide a selection of fiction from the class library. Ask the children to look at the openings of each story and group the books according to how they open.

■ Call the children back as a group and discuss their findings. Were there any story openings they could not sort into the four hooks? Which story openings made them want to continue reading?

INDEPENDENT WRITING ACTIVITY
■ Remind the children about the characters they invented in 'Star characters'.

■ Ask them to write four different paragraphs to open a story for their character, using the four hooks. Tell them not to worry about the plot or what will happen next at this time, but to concentrate on grabbing the reader's attention.

PLENARY
■ Ask the children to read their openings aloud. Discuss the impression each different one gives. How different are they? Which ones work best for their character? Which story opening do they want to use again? Encourage them to remember and develop openings that they could use in the SATs test.

Story openings

At the time the strangers came, the Manth people were still living in the low-walled shelters that they had carried with them in their hunting days. The domed huts were clustered around the salt mine that was to become the source of their wealth.

Text © William Nicholson

The tiger padded through the night, Joe Maloney smelt it, the hot sour breath, the stench of its pelt. The odour crept through the streets, through his open window and into his dreams.

Text © David Almond

'I can't choose anything,' wailed Bonny, tossing the brochure on the floor. 'Not out of this horrible lot. Why can't I just stay here?'

Text © Anne Fine

I would never have had the courage for it myself. It was my cousin Harry who did it. She was eleven when she did it, and I was eleven when she told me about it; though by that time she was nearly grown-up herself.

Text © Jill Paton-Walsh

PLANS

OBJECTIVE
To use figurative language to describe a stock character.

YOU WILL NEED
Photocopiable page 23.

In this session the children explore the use of metaphor and simile to describe their characters. This means they will build up a bank they can re-use in the test situation and help them raise the standard of their writing.

WHOLE CLASS ACTIVITY

■ Tell the children that in this session they are going to practise giving depth and interest to their writing by using simile and metaphor. Explain that writers sometimes compare an ordinary thing with something unusual, to create an interesting or striking image.

■ Recap that a simile compares one thing with another, using 'as' or 'like' ('Hair as curly as lamb's wool'). A metaphor says that one thing actually is another ('His hair was a tangle of barbed wire').

■ Write some colour words on the board and ask the children to suggest similes for each (for example, 'as blue as...', 'black like...' and so on). Encourage them to make unusual comparisons rather than commonplace ones such as 'black as coal' and so on.

■ Explain that some metaphors and similes have become so overused that they have become clichés and will not seem at all interesting or imaginative. They should avoid them 'like the plague'!

■ Write the following nouns on the board: branches, wind, sun, moon, snow, daffodils. Write a comparison for one of the nouns (e.g. 'branches like bony fingers'). Suggest that this is perhaps an overused simile, but that extending it might add interest.

■ Demonstrate how to change the simile into a metaphor (for example, 'The bony fingers of the trees...'). Ask the children to suggest what the branches might do that fingers do (for example, scratch, wave, click).

■ Demonstrate how to extend the metaphor using their suggestions (for example, The bony fingers of the tree scratched the window pane.')

■ Ask the children to collect the work they have done previously on their characters, and to work with a partner. Ask them to compare each other's characters and together, to draw up a list of physical appearances and characteristics of personality they can use in metaphors and similes.

POINTS

Preparing metaphors and similes for their characters in advance will make writing them in the SATs writing paper quicker and easier, and add greater interest to their writing.

DON'T PANIC!
■ If any children have difficulty, partner them with another child and ask them to brainstorm ideas together for each character, taking one character at a time.

INDEPENDENT WRITING ACTIVITY

■ Ask the children to use photocopiable page 23 to create as many metaphors and similes as they can to use for their stock character's appearance. If time allows, ask them to repeat it for personalities.

PLENARY

■ Ask the children to choose which metaphors and similes they think work best and read them aloud. Ask the children to say how they feel about using metaphor and simile in their character descriptions. Discuss whether this has improved the image of their character, and if it has given them depth.

Metaphor and simile

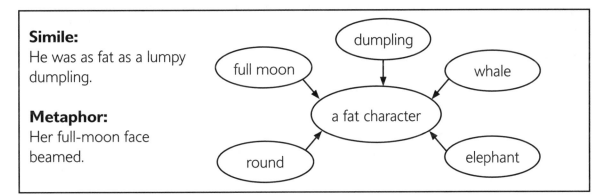

Simile:
He was as fat as a lumpy dumpling.

Metaphor:
Her full-moon face beamed.

dumpling
full moon
whale
a fat character
round
elephant

■ Use a pencil to write something about your character in the centre of the web, then add as many images as you can, as in the example above.
■ Use them to create a simile and a metaphor. Re-use the web with other characteristics such as thin, tall, beautiful, ugly, lazy, happy and so on.

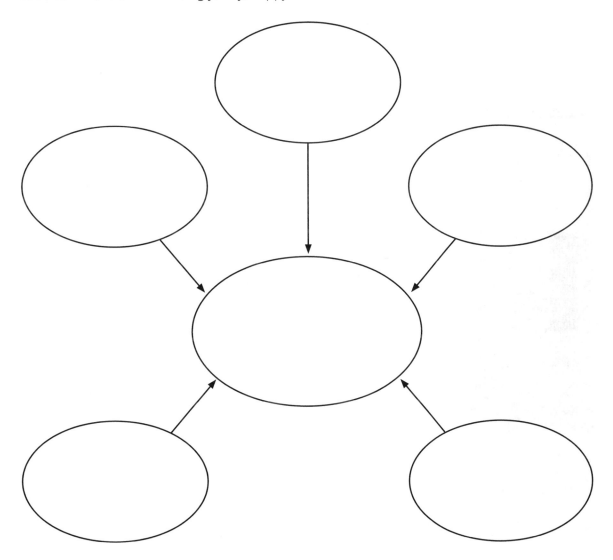

QUICK FIX FOR YEAR 6: **WRITING**

SETTING DESCRIPTIONS

Children can achieve better marks for their story writing if they include effective and relevant descriptions using the senses: sight, sound, touch, smell and taste. They will also achieve higher marks when they can manipulate their sentence structures to provide variety, showing how the sentences can affect the mood and atmosphere of their writing.

OBJECTIVE
To write setting descriptions that are precise and relevant.

WHAT YOU NEED
Photocopiable page 25, highlighter pens.

WHOLE CLASS ACTIVITY

■ Ask the children to work with a partner and brainstorm three or more reasons for including descriptions of settings in their writing.

■ Gather the children back as a group and discuss their findings. If no one has identified 'letting readers experience the setting' or similar, explain that good writing 'involves' the reader and makes them see, hear and feel what the author imagines.

■ Ask the children to suggest which senses they could use to describe a setting, and draw up a list: sight, sound, touch, smell, taste. Point out that good writing also portrays the feelings of the character. Readers will be more involved if they feel the way the character feels about the setting.

■ Hand out photocopiable page 25 to each pair. Ask the pairs to read the two setting descriptions. Tell them to identify how the extracts are similar and different, which senses are used in the descriptions, and discuss how the settings make them feel, and why. Ask them what impression the word 'mournful' makes on the second description.

■ Gather the children back together and take feedback. Discuss the use of descriptive noun phrases. Ask them to identify the adjectives in both passages. Point out how the use of adjectives is precise. Explain that overuse of unnecessary description can detract from the effect of your writing and make readers lose interest.

■ Tell the children to work with their partners again and explore the sentence structures used in each extract. Ask them to identify where the authors have used a variety of structures: complex and compound sentences, varied sentence beginnings, varied punctuation. Ask them to identify the use of simile and metaphor and highlight these.

MAIN POINTS
Precise vocabulary can help keep description relevant. Overuse of adjectives can lose marks. Careful use of simile and metaphor can create memorable images and raise marks. Make use of the senses of sound, sight, smell and touch.

DON'T PANIC!
■ If children need extra support, tell them to limit their descriptions to only two senses.

INDEPENDENT WRITING ACTIVITY

■ Tell the children to imagine that their familiar characters are in a wood. Explain that you want the children to write two different setting descriptions. The first should have a calm, friendly atmosphere, and the second should be tense and frightening. Tell them to try and give an impression (show, not tell) of how their character feels about the setting, and to remember to make use of the senses. Remind them to keep their use of descriptive phrases precise and relevant to their character and setting. Encourage them to use short, sharp sentences to heighten tension, and long sentences to slow down the pace.

■ In pairs, the children should take turns to read one description each, and the other should comment on whether it has a calm or tense atmosphere.

PLENARY

■ Ask the children to read their descriptions aloud. Compare the calm descriptions with the tense ones. Ask the children to say which are most effective and give reasons. Praise those who have varied their sentence structures and punctuation, and used figurative language sparingly but effectively. Explain that this will result in higher marks in their tests.

Descriptive settings

From the moment he entered it the wood seemed full of noises. There was a smell of damp leaves and moss, and everywhere the splash of water went whispering about. Just inside, the brook made a little fall into a pool and the sound, enclosed among the trees, echoed as though in a cave. Roosting birds rustled overhead; the night breeze stirred the leaves; here and there a dead twig fell. And there were more sinister, unidentified sounds, from further away; sounds of movement.

Text © Richard Adams

The grass in the field had been heavy with dew, but the ground was dry under close growing trees. There were very few tall, thick trunks. Most were spindly with several narrow stems shooting up from the same spot. The wood was so quiet that every movement Peter made seemed unnaturally loud. Even the slight swishing sound of dead leaves stirred by his feet seemed to carry a long way. The air was still, and there was no breeze to rustle the leaves. The birds, too, seemed to have fallen silent, though he could hear the mournful cawing of crows, some distance away.

Text © Elizabeth Laird

A SENSE OF SOUND

OBJECTIVE
To use poetic devices in stories.

WHAT YOU NEED
Photocopiable pages 27, 28 and 29.

In this lesson the children will be examining a piece of text by David Almond to identify how the author has used imagery, rhythm and alliteration to create an atmospheric setting and vivid prose. They will explore different poetic devices and try to use some of them in their own writing.

WHOLE CLASS ACTIVITY
■ Give each child a copy of photocopiable page 27. Ask them to read it to themselves.

■ Working in pairs ask the children to describe the setting briefly in their own words to each other, thinking about Who? What? Where?

■ Next, ask them to discuss how the extract makes them feel. Does it give them a 'physical' feeling? How would they feel if they were in the same setting? Ask them to picture it in their heads.

■ Ask what sort of story they think this comes from and to find evidence in the text to support their opinions. Who is the narrator? Ask them to look at the first line and suggest who 'him' might refer to. How has this person affected the narrator's opinion and feelings about the setting?

■ Read the noun-phrases in the first sentence aloud with the children, emphasising the hard sounds of the consonants, particularly 'dilapidated quays' and 'broken buildings'. Ask the children to suggest why the author chose these adjectives and nouns.

■ Write the sentence on the board, beginning with ' The dark alleyways' as if it were a verse from a poem, for example:

The dark alleyways
The dilapidated quays
The broken buildings
The place he said was mad, was evil
The place he said was death.

■ Discuss how, when writing poetry, a poet says a great deal in few words. Explain that authors often use imagery and poetic devices that convey much to the reader using few words. Explain that this technique can help them give layers of meaning to their writing, especially in a timed situation, such as the SATs writing paper.

■ Tell them to go through the text together and underline any striking images, repetitions and imaginative words and phrases. What effect do they have on the sounds and images of the writing? Ask them to identify alliteration, same or similar vowel sounds (assonance), metaphor, rhythmical sentence structures, unusual contrasts (oxymoron).

MAIN POINTS

Using poetic devices in writing prose can help children give layers of meaning to their writing and move beyond the literal in few words. Poetic devices can make writing more vivid by putting memorable images in the reader's mind.

DON'T PANIC!
■ For children who have difficulty understanding the difference in the poetic devices, enlarge the list on photocopiable page 28 and display it.
■ An annotated copy of the text (on photocopiable page 29) can be used for further support.

INDEPENDENT WRITING ACTIVITY
■ Mask the bottom half of photocopiable page 28 and provide each pair of children with a copy. Ask them to write a list of nouns associated with each setting, and experiment with creating alliterative phrases, onomatopoeia and oxymoron that they could use in their own writing. Give them a thesaurus to help them experiment with alternative words.

PLENARY
■ Ask some of the children to read their images aloud while others identify which poetic device they have used. Ask them to identify which they feel are the strongest and best images. Give extra praise for children who have used unusual contrasts and included metaphor.

■ Ask the children to record their best poetic phrases in their writing notebooks to help them remember them for future use.

I left him and turned back to the dark alleyways, the dilapidated quays, the broken buildings, the ruins of the past, the place he said was mad, was evil, the place he said was death. I kicked my way through ancient litter and fallen rubble. The walls and ceilings creaked and groaned. Dust seethed all around me. Shadows shifted. Dark birds flapped above. Dangling doors led into pitch-black rooms and offices. The ground was cracked and potholed. In places it had simply fallen away, and yawning gaps showed cavernous cellars below. I imagined ghosts all around me, watching me, the ghosts of those who had worked here and filled the place with noise and light and life. I felt their fingers touching me as I walked, heard their hollow breathing, their whispering, their sad laughter.

Text © David Almond

Atmospheric settings

■ Write phrases to use for a description of the following settings, using poetic devices to create interesting images.

Setting 1: The coast
Suggestions to start you off: cliffs, coves, coast, sea, sand, shells, fish, froth, foam

_____

_____

_____

Setting 2: Forest
Suggestions to start you off: fir, forest, pine, deep, dark, dapple, boughs, beams, bracken

_____

_____

_____

Setting 3: City
Suggestions to start you off: Skyscraper, suburb, stories, subway, heat, houses, metal, mansion, traffic, tram, train

_____

_____

_____

Alliteration The repetition of initial sounds: <u>d</u>angling <u>d</u>oors; <u>b</u>roken <u>b</u>uildings; <u>sh</u>adows <u>sh</u>ifted

Assonance The close repetition of vowel sounds: gh<u>o</u>sts of th<u>o</u>se; l<u>i</u>ght and l<u>i</u>fe

Onomatopoeia Words whose sounds suggest their meanings: creaked and groaned; seethed

Oxymoron Combining two contradicting words in one phrase: sad laughter

Rhythm Grouping words in a phrase or sentence so that the stress on syllables creates a rhythm: The **walls** and **ceil**ings creaked and groaned; The **ground** was **cracked** and **pot**holed; With **noise** and **light** and **life**

I left him and turned back to the dark alleyways, the [(1)] dilapidated quays, the broken buildings, the ruins of the past, [(2)] the place he said was mad, was evil, the place he said was death. I kicked my way through ancient litter and fallen rubble. [(3)] The walls and ceilings creaked and groaned. Dust [(4)] seethed all around me. Shadows shifted. Dark birds flapped above. [(5)] Dangling doors led into pitch-black rooms and offices. [(3)] The ground was cracked and potholed. In places it had simply fallen away, and yawning gaps showed cavernous cellars below. I imagined ghosts all around me, watching me, the [(6)] ghosts of those who had worked here and filled the place with noise and [(6)] light and life. I felt their fingers touching me as I walked, heard their hollow breathing, their whispering, their [(7)] sad laughter.

[(1)] hard sounds of consonants gives a harsh tone

[(2)] repetition

[(3)] repeated pattern of rhythmical sentence structure

[(4)] metaphor

onomatopoeia

[(5)] alliteration

[(3)] repeated pattern of rhythmical sentence structure

[(6)] assonance, repeated vowel sound

[(7)] oxymoron: contradicting words

Text © David Almond

WHAT A DILEMMA!

OBJECTIVE
To create a problem for a character in order to develop the plot.

WHAT YOU NEED
Photocopiable page 31.

MAIN POINTS

A story needs characters to face a dilemma or problem in order to be interesting. Practice in planning simple dilemmas and problems will help children understand the need to plan before they begin writing, which will make it easier for them to write a convincing story in their tests.

DON'T PANIC!
■ If children need extra support, ask them to re-read the extract from *The Power of One* on photocopiable page 11 and identify what went wrong for the main character.

In this session the children learn about four different problems or dilemmas that characters can face to give an interesting plot in their stories. If the children familiarise themselves with plot structures their stories will have a good structure and gain higher marks in the SATs writing paper.

WHOLE CLASS ACTIVITY
■ Read a simple nursery rhyme to the children, for example 'Mary, Mary, Quite Contrary':
Mary, Mary, quite contrary, how does your garden grow?
With silver bells and cockle shells and pretty maids all in a row.
■ Explain the structure as a narrative story, for example, Mary has got a garden in which she wants to grow lots of flowers and decorate it with silver bells and seashells. She succeeds. The end.
■ Ask the children if this would make an interesting or exciting story or not, and why. You should elicit what is wrong, for example, nothing goes wrong; there is no dilemma so Mary does not have to make important decisions or overcome difficulties. Make a few suggestions for dilemmas that she could face, for example, giant slugs from outer space arrive at night, eat everything and trap her in the potting shed.
■ Ask the children to work with a partner and discuss what can go wrong in stories to give the characters a dilemma, or problem to solve. Tell them to think of simple situations, not specific details, and to let their imaginations run riot.
■ Gather the children back in a group and discuss their findings. Make a note of some of their suggested problems on the board. If the children do not suggest the following, explain that there are four simple dilemmas they can use when writing an adventure story:
Something/someone is lost
Someone is chased
Someone/something is trapped
Someone needs to get somewhere else.

INDEPENDENT WRITING ACTIVITY
■ Explain that the children are going to use their familiar character and write four different dilemmas for them to face. Give them a single scene or setting to use for their character (for example, going to play in a vital cup game; getting a part in the school play).
■ Demonstrate on the board using one scenario (for exapmle, X wants the lead role in the school play. So does Y. Auditions. X misses the bus and is too late. Y gets the part).
■ Ask the children to make notes on photocopiable page 31 (using their planned character and one of the four dilemmas) of a plot for an adventure story in your chosen setting. Tell the children not to worry about solving the problem yet but to concentrate on creating an interesting dilemma.
■ Tell them to swap with a partner and discuss each other's plans. Which ones work? Which one will best suit the particular character?

PLENARY
■ Ask some of the children to use their notes to tell the class about their character's dilemmas.
■ Ask the children which dilemma they preferred to use for their own character, and discuss their choices and reasons.

Adventure story writing frame

■ Write your character's name and make notes about what will happen next.

Lost _____
Trapped _____
Chased _____
Trying to get somewhere _____

PLANNING YOUR STORY

This session gives children an understanding of the need to think about the ending of their story in the planning stage. This is essential for getting high marks in the writing tasks of the SATs writing paper. More marks are given when it is clear that the child has planned out their plot before beginning so that it is well structured and cohesive.

WHOLE CLASS TEACHING
■ Explain to the children the importance of having a plan before they start writing a story. They will get better marks if they plan first, and then stick to it. It is better to write a short, carefully structured piece of writing than a long, rambling story.
■ Explain that a plan does not need to be complete sentences, but simple brief notes.
■ Remind them of different planning approaches such as flow-charts, diagrams, story-staircases, story-mountains or whatever they are familiar with.
■ Remind the children of the writing they have done before on character, openings and dilemmas. Ask them to suggest the essential elements needed for planning and draw up a list of headings (for example, opening, build-up of events, dilemma or problem, resolution, ending).
■ Illustrate how to use notes to plan a story about a hungry mouse, while asking the children:
   Who is the main character? (a mouse)
   What is the setting? (a kitchen)
   What is the problem? (how to reach the cheese without getting caught)
   How is the problem solved?
   What is the ending?
■ Explain to the children that when they think of the problem, they should think about how to solve it at the same time, or they will not be able to end the story.
■ Tell them to avoid lazy endings, such as: '…and they all went home.'; '…and then I woke up.'; 'The end.' Using these will lower their marks.
■ A good tip for ending a story: refer to the opening and re-use some of the vocabulary and sentence structure. For example, begin with 'Milly Mouse hadn't seen any cheese for days and days' and end with 'It was days and days before she wanted to see cheese again.'

INDEPENDENT WRITING ACTIVITY
■ Ask the children to work with a partner and use photocopiable page 33 to make notes on a plan for a short story, using their familiar character. Remind them about the dilemmas they wrote in 'What a dilemma!'. Tell them to discuss in pairs which dilemma to use for their character and how to solve it. Ask them to make notes of the basic elements and add any details around the bubbles.
■ Ask them to describe their story plans to a partner, then to swap and comment on each other's story from their plan. Encourage them to discuss particularly how the problem in the plot is solved and the plan for the ending.

PLENARY
■ Ask the children to describe their partner's stories and discuss how effective the planning notes were. Is the problem resolved? Can they improve the ending?

Story planner

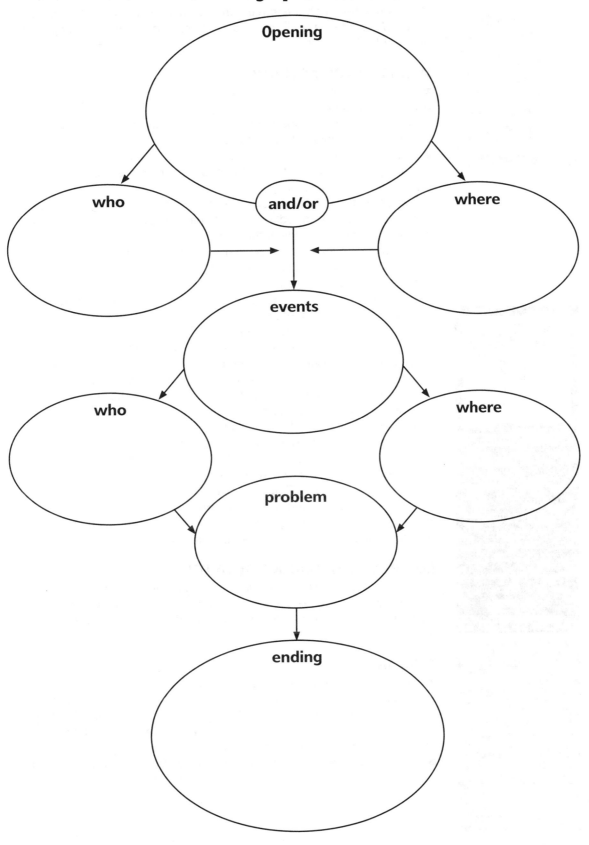

PLAYSCRIPT

OBJECTIVE
To use an existing piece of work as a basis for writing a play script.

WHAT YOU NEED
Photocopiable pages 7 and 35.

Play scripts follow a set of conventions that are different from narrative fiction. When children understand how to use dialogue and stage directions they will feel more confident about conveying a scene through the characters' dialogue.

DON'T PANIC!
■ If children have difficulty turning their writing into a play script, tell them to go through their writing with a coloured pen and highlight the characters and their spoken words using different colours for different characters.

Children need to be familiar with playscripts so that they don't panic if asked to write one. If they are familiar with the similarities and differences between narrative fiction and scriptwriting conventions, they will be able to write a more confident and lively playscript and achieve higher marks.

WHOLE CLASS ACTIVITY
■ Ask the children to brainstorm in pairs a list of the layout features of a playscript and a story.
■ Gather the children together again and draw up two lists on the board to compare and contrast the features.
■ Discuss the common features, for example both tell a story with a beginning, series of events, a plot, complication and resolution. Both include action and dialogue.
■ Encourage the children to describe the key distinguishing features of a playscript: a cast list introduces all the characters at the beginning; the setting is described briefly at the beginning of each scene; the plot is conveyed to the audience through dialogue; each time a character speaks, his or her name is listed on the left of the page; no speech marks or reporting clauses are used.
■ Explain the function of the stage director if needed. Ask the children to suggest how a stage director conveys to the actors how to speak the dialogue, and what actions to take.
■ Give pairs of children a copy of photocopiable page 7 and the playscript on photocopiable page 35. Ask them to read both texts. Explain that the first scene of the playscript is annotated to show script conventions. Encourage them to discuss how to add directions to the second scene of the playscript to make it more energetic and convey how the characters speak and behave. Ask them to think carefully about if and when to add annotations to the dialogue in the play script. Ask them to use a different colour pen and annotate the second scene to show the conventions of playscripts, as done in the first scene.
■ Rearrange the children into groups of three. Ask them to use their annotated playscripts and act out the two scenes.
■ Gather them together again to discuss whether their annotated directions helped them read the script with more expression.

INDEPENDENT WRITING ACTIVITY
■ Ask the children to choose a piece of fiction they have written previously, that includes dialogue. Ask them to turn it into a play script using the conventions and features identified in the earlier part of the lesson.

PLENARY
■ Invite the children to swap playscripts with each other and discuss their writing. Ask them to comment on what works, what could be improved and how. For example, have they laid out the script correctly? Did they remember not to use speech marks? Have they made sure the stage directions are not mistaken for part of the dialogue?
■ Ask some of the children to form a cast and act out some of their plays.

Playscript

Cast:
Tom (about 12)
Rosie (a girl about 10)
Jess (about 6)

Scene 1

A sandy beach with rocks and cliffs to one side. Three children, Tom, Jess and Rosie enter stage left. Rosie runs to the edge of the sea and then back and forward in the waves while shrieking with delight.

Notes about the scene are written at the beginning using italics

Tom: *(irritated)* Jess! Grow up, for goodness sake!

Jess continues running back and forward.

Jess: *(shrieking)* Whoah! Whee!

The way a character speaks is written inside brackets in italics

Tom: I'm bored.

Rosie: Look, Tom. Jess! Come on. We're going to explore the cliffs.

She runs off stage right, the others follow.

Stage directions are written in italics, in the present tense

Scene 2

Rosie: Wow! It's a cave!

Tom: Don't go in, Rosie.

A new line is used for a new speaker

Rosie: Oh, don't be such a wimp! I thought you were bored. Come on Jess.

Jess: It looks very dark in there.

Rose: It's a smugglers' cave. We might find some treasure. I'm going in.

Tom: We were told to stay together. I'm the oldest. I'll go first.

They enter the cave...

SCHOLASTIC
www.scholastic.co.uk

QUICK FIX FOR YEAR 6: **WRITING**

TELLING TALES

Fairy tales, fables, myths and legends come from the tradition of passing on stories orally. Many have been written down but still retain a particular voice, often addressing the reader personally. They have many features in common but certain key differences. Children need to be prepared to write in the style asked for in the SATs writing paper in order to achieve high marks. In this lesson, they compare and contrast examples of each genre and write their own version of a folk tale or myth.

WHOLE CLASS ACTIVITY
■ Discuss what the children already know about the typical characters and plots of folk tales, fairy tales, fables and myths with the children. Brainstorm a list of features and write it on the board. For example: animals with human characteristics; magical people or creatures; gods or supernatural beings; a moral; story-teller language such as 'Once upon a time' and 'Once, long ago'.
■ Ask the children to work with a partner and explore the selection of books, classifying them according to genre using Post-it notes. If a story has already been classified by another pair, encourage them to check that they agree with the choice. Ask the pairs of children to choose one fairy tale or folk tale, one fable and one myth, and make notes of the features that identify the genre for each story.
■ Gather the children together and review the brainstormed list of features in light of the paired activity. Ask each pair to suggest one key feature that stands out to denote the genre. For example: Fairy tales and folk tales – magic; Fables – animals or inanimate objects behaving as humans; Myths – supernatural beings or gods.
■ Provide the children with the photocopiable pages 37 and 38, and ask them to read the opening of *The Nightingale* aloud to each other, and to identify any features of story-teller language in the text, such as addressing the reader personally and repetition of key phrases. Then ask them to tell each other the fable and the myth on photocopiable page 38 in their own words. Encourage them to use the style of narration in The Nightingale; addressing their listener and using repetition for effect.
■ Gather the children together again and discuss how their oral retellings differ from the written stories. Ask them to describe the storytelling techniques they used.

INDEPENDENT WRITING ACTIVITY
■ Ask the children to work with their partner and write their own full version of either *The Workman and the Nightingale*, or *The Story of Orpheus*. Tell them to write it as a story to be told aloud.
■ Invite them to swap and read the stories aloud to each other.

PLENARY
■ Ask the children to describe how the language and style of their myths or fables differs from the stories they have written previously.
■ Discuss how effective they were and identify which ones worked best and why.

THE NIGHTINGALE

A good story ripens with age and constant telling. It sings in the heart, like the sweet song of the nightingale cuts through even the darkest night. Although the Emperor of China, where this story comes from and who ruled without question over all his subjects, including the little nightingale, might disagree.

The Emperor lived in the most magnificent Palace made of the finest porcelain, as delicate and fragile as beaten gold. By day, the sunlight shone through its translucent walls, bathing the airy rooms with fragrant light. By night, the moon shone its silvery beams into even the darkest corners.

Outside, the Palace gardens unfolded like an intricate hand-woven carpet. And, just as a good story blossoms and matures with each telling, so the Emperor's garden revealed more ingenious surprises as it stretched down through enchanting woodland to the blue ocean. Exotic flowers with tiny silver bells tied to them, filled the air with their perfume and a rich tapestry of silvery sound. It was truly a wonder! The Emperor looked at his work and was proud.

A lowly fisherman would watch the Emperor's great ships sail near the shore as he cast his net out into the blueness of the ocean. He too would marvel at the Emperor's work, but the hardness of his life and the constant casting of his nets would make him forget everything. Then the nightingale would sing and lift the fisherman's heart with her sweet song. It was truly a wonder!

Travellers came from far and wide to marvel at the Emperor's Palace and the beauty of his gardens. When they returned home, they wrote of all the wonders they had seen in the Emperor's vast and beautiful land. But the most vivid descriptions, the most vibrant poems, were kept for the nightingale.

These books came, eventually, even as far as the great land of China. The Emperor would nod his head with delight as he read eagerly about his great wonders and was proud. Then he read, 'But the greatest wonder in all the Emperor's great land is the nightingale.'

Text © Campbell Perry

Name _____

The Workman and the Nightingale

One summer night, a workman passed a wood on his way home. He stopped to listen to a nightingale singing, and stayed listening for hours. He was so delighted with the sound that the next night he set a trap for it and captured it. "Now I've caught you," he cried, "you shall sing only for me!"

"I can never sing in a cage," said the nightingale sadly.

"Then I may as well eat you," said the workman. "Nightingale on toast will be a fine supper!"

"Pray, do not kill me," said the nightingale. "Set me free and I promise to tell you three things that are far better than eating me." So the workman set the nightingale free. He flew up to the branch of a tree and said: "The first thing I have to tell you is this: never believe what a captive promises you; the second is: keep hold of what you have; and finally: don't sorrow over what is gone forever!" And the nightingale flew away.

Retold by Gillian Howell

Orpheus and Eurydice

Orpheus was so deeply in love with his wife Eurydice that he played and sang to her as beautifully as a nightingale. His songs charmed wild beasts and calmed storms. But when a snake bit Eurydice and she died, Orpheus was overcome with grief. He wandered the forests singing mournful songs filled with grief and longing.

Orpheus pleaded with the god of the Underworld to let Eurydice return. So great was the power of his music that Pluto, the god of the Underworld, agreed on one condition; Orpheus must lead his wife up from the Underworld and not look back at her even once. Then just as he neared the top of the journey up from the Underworld, Orpheus was tempted to see if she really was following him; and he looked back. There he saw Eurydice disappearing back down the dark tunnel, back down into the Underworld.

Orpheus's grief was overwhelming. Once again he wandered the forests, mourning his lost love and he never loved again. Even the beautiful women of Thrace could not tempt him. In their fury at his rejection, they killed him.

His bones were buried at the foot of Mount Olympus, and even today, the song of the nightingales over his grave is the most beautiful on Earth.

Retold by Gillian Howell

Planning frame

The characters (*who they are and why they are special*)

The setting (*what and how is it important to this story?*)

Story-teller words and phrases (*long, long, ago... / as you know... / and that is why...*)
Add some more of your own

Ideas for repetition

Ideas for ending (*And to this day... / From then on...*)
Add some more of your own

LESSON PLANS

OBJECTIVE
To describe past events in chronological order.

WHAT YOU NEED
Photocopiable pages 41, 42 and 43, highlighter and marker pens.

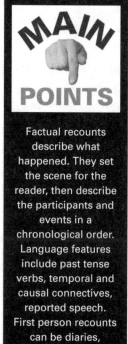

MAIN POINTS

Factual recounts describe what happened. They set the scene for the reader, then describe the participants and events in a chronological order. Language features include past tense verbs, temporal and causal connectives, reported speech. First person recounts can be diaries, biographies, letters and newspaper eyewitness accounts.

DON'T PANIC!
■ Support children who need it with the recount writing frame on photocopiable page 43 to help them organise their ideas before writing and to remind them of the features of a recount. An annotated copy of the extract is available on page 42 gives further help.

In this lesson, children examine the structure and form of a typical first-person recount. They identify key facts and events, temporal connectives, cause and effect in order to write a short recount of the passage in their own words. These are key skills that will enable them to interpret text and summarise in their own words in a test situation. In later lessons they explore other forms of recount, including journalism, letter and diary writing. Children will achieve higher marks in their SATs writing paper when they can automatically use the structures and language styles of different recounts.

WHOLE CLASS ACTIVITY
■ Hand out photocopiable page 41 and ask the children to read the extract. Encourage them to think about what sort of extract it is while they read. Discuss what sort of text they think it is; fiction or non-fiction. Brainstorm types of recount with the children, and identify into which category this text falls (autobiography).
■ Brainstorm the main features of a first-person recount and draw up a list (introduction, consistent past tense verbs, chronological order, reported rather than direct speech). Remind the children to think of What? Who? Where? When? How? and Why?
■ Ask the children to work with a partner and mark up the text to identify the following features: setting the scene, key events, facts used to give information and add interest, statements of feelings or personal opinions, temporal connectives, language of cause and effect, reported speech.
■ Gather the children back into a group and discuss their findings.
■ Ask some of them to summarise the extract orally. Discuss their summaries with the other children and ask them to comment on the key events and information they included. Were they needed for understanding the events described in the text? Was anything important missed out?
■ Ask the children to work with a partner again to each write a summary of the text in less than six sentences. Tell them to swap their summaries and to compare and contrast what each had included as key to the recount.
■ Ask some of the children to read their summaries aloud and discuss whether they had retained interest for readers. Brainstorm what is needed to make their recounts more interesting for readers.

INDEPENDENT WRITING ACTIVITY
■ Ask the children to use their partner's summary as a basis and rewrite it as a first-person recount, as if they were the child in the autobiography. Ask them to include anything they think is needed to add interest, using their memory of the extract but writing in their own words.
■ Remind the children to write the key events in chronological order, to vary their sentence structures, as this will really help them raise the standard of their writing. Encourage them to use interesting connectives to link the events, and to close the recount with a statement about how they felt or why it was important.

PLENARY
■ Ask the children to read their recounts aloud and identify what aspects are good and what could be improved.
■ Discuss how their recounts differ from the extract on which they are based.

In June the following year I left to spend a holiday with friends on the isle of Lewis in the Outer Hebrides. The weather throughout my stay was very rough. Walking along the beach one morning to collect pieces of driftwood, I saw a fisherman coming towards me carrying an oddly shaped creature in his arms. He told me it was a young seal which had probably got washed off its rock during the night by the gale and separated from its mother. Many young seals are lost in this manner. What was a little unusual was the fact that it was a Common Seal, a species more often found on the East Coast, the Hebrides being the breeding ground of the larger, less intelligent Atlantic Seal. Although my knowledge of seal upbringing was of the scantiest, I promptly asked the fisherman if I might have it, and, greatly to my joy, he placed the seal in my arms. A bottle was presented to me by a kindly woman and I was instructed how to fill it with warmed milk mixed with a little oil. Seals' milk is very rich, containing almost ten times more fat than cows' milk. Lora, as I had named her, took to the bottle without fuss and showed every prospect of thriving. She became very tame almost from the start and enjoyed being handled and stroked.

Animal lover though I knew Aunt Miriam to be, I decided after some thought not to inform her in my letter that I had become the owner of a young Common Seal, but to take my pet back unannounced as a 'surprise', trusting that Lora's affectionate nature would win Aunt over to the realisation that a home without a seal lacks a vital member of the family party.

A fortnight later I set off on the two days' journey home with Lora, a somewhat bulky parcel weighing over thirty-eight pounds, wrapped up in a tartan rug.

Extract from Seal Morning by Rowena Farre

SCHOLASTIC
www.scholastic.co.uk

Name _____

DON'T PANIC!

In June the following year I left to spend a holiday with friends on the isle of Lewis in the Outer Hebrides. The weather throughout my stay was very rough. Walking along the beach one morning to collect pieces of driftwood, I saw a fisherman coming towards me carrying an oddly shaped creature in his arms. He told me it was a young seal which had probably got washed off its rock during the night by the gale and separated from its mother. Many young seals are lost in this manner. What was a little unusual was the fact that it was a Common Seal, a species more often found on the East Coast, the Hebrides being the breeding ground of the larger, less intelligent Atlantic Seal. Although my knowledge of seal upbringing was of the scantiest, I promptly asked the fisherman if I might have it, and, greatly to my joy, he placed the seal in my arms. A bottle was presented to me by a kindly woman and I was instructed how to fill it with warmed milk mixed with a little oil. Seals' milk is very rich, containing almost ten times more fat than cows' milk. Lora, as I had named her, took to the bottle without fuss and showed every prospect of thriving. She became very tame almost from the start and enjoyed being handled and stroked.

Animal lover though I knew Aunt Miriam to be, I decided after some thought not to inform her in my letter that I had become the owner of a young Common Seal, but to take my pet back unannounced as a 'surprise', trusting that Lora's affectionate nature would win Aunt over to the realisation that a home without a seal lacks a vital member of the family party.

A fortnight later I set off on the two days' journey home with Lora, a somewhat bulky parcel weighing over thirty-eight pounds, wrapped up in a tartan rug.

opening statement: 'What?'

'who?': first person

'where?'

past tense verbs

first event

reported speech

interesting factual detail

cause and effect connective

reported speech
second event

third event

interesting detail

sequence of cause and effect

concluding event

temporal connective

detail adds interest

Extract from Seal Morning by Rowena Farre

Planning frame

Who is involved?

Where does it take place?

What happens?	**Who says what?**

Feelings?

Connecting words and phrases	**Conclusion**

READ ALL ABOUT IT!

In this lesson, the children continue to explore the features and conventions of recount writing. Becoming familiar with the consistent features of recounts will mean they can confidently use them to write a recount in any style that features in their SATs writing paper.

WHOLE CLASS ACTIVITY

■ Hand out photocopiable page 45.

■ Read the text together and discuss what sort of text it is. Point out that, although this is written in the style of a newspaper report, it is recounting events that have happened in the past. Brainstorm the features of the text that are typical of a recount, for example, introduction/scene-setting, past tense verbs, chronological order, reported speech.

■ Ask the children to describe the key features in the writing that are specific to a journalistic style and draw up a list, for example, headline, sub-heading, introductory sentence, passive sentences, quotations, statistics, paragraphing and layout, sensational words, fact and opinion.

■ Ask the children to work with a partner to annotate the text, marking up the key features of journalistic writing according to their list.

■ Gather the children back into a group. Discuss the purpose of the text with the children. Ask them if the main subject of the recount is the children, or the lifeboat service (the lifeboat service). Ask them to identify any devices used to draw the reader into the text, for example, headlines, subheadings and bold print to grab readers' attention.

■ Focus on the quotations and how the spoken words differ from the previous recount text (direct speech rather than reported speech). Identify the different reporting clauses and verbs to describe speech. Ask why the writer has used verbs such as 'commented', 'added' and 'described'. Discuss how extra details about the people involved, such as their ages, add interest to the recount.

■ Ask the children to point out facts and opinions. Discuss reasons for including opinions in journalistic recounts. Introduce the idea that opinions in newspaper reports can sometimes be disguised, to influence the reader without them realising it.

■ Draw attention to the verbs and tenses. Explain how the account of what happened uses the past tense consistently, but where comments are made, by the writer or quotes from witnesses, the tenses change. Ask them to identify where the passive voice is used and the effect.

■ Note how the subheadings and paragraphs are used to organise the information.

INDEPENDENT WRITING ACTIVITY

■ Ask the children to write a newspaper report describing a rescue. They could use the text on photocopiable page 7 as a stimulus for ideas. Explain that they should choose an effective headline, and model the layout on Rescue At Sea! Ask them to include quotations from the people involved and from eyewitnesses.

PLENARY

■ Choose some of the children to read their pieces aloud. Find which pieces were most effective and ask the children why they were. Identify areas for improvement, for example: Are verb tenses used accurately? Is sufficient detail included to interest the reader? Is it easy to see what the article is about - are there effective sub-headings to lead the reader?

Daily Clarion, Thursday March 30, 2006

Rescue at sea!

Dramatic scenes occurred on Wednesday night when the storm of the century hit the Atlantic coast. Loss of life was narrowly averted.

Children in Rescue Drama

THE OFF-SHORE LIFEBOAT SERVICE was once again at the centre of a dramatic rescue when it was called out last Wednesday night. Three children had been spotted drifting out to sea by a passer-by. They were in a small boat as the weather deteriorated. They were named as Jack Morris (10), Jonas Leech (10) and Sam Patel (11).

Stunned

"I couldn't believe my eyes," said Trevor Jones (67), a local resident who raised the alarm. "I'd come to watch the storm from the cliffs and I saw them being washed away. I called 999 from my mobile phone and alerted the coast guard. They had no sails or oars," added Mr Jones, "and were being battered by the storm."

The lifeboat was raised at 7.45pm and reached the children at 8pm. During a risky operation to transfer the children to safety, one of the lifeboat crew was almost swept overboard as waves reaching 15 feet threatened to swamp both craft.

Heroes

"I can't thank the lifeboat service enough!" said Mrs Sandra Morris, mother of one of the boys. "These people are true heroes. You can be sure the boys will never be so stupid again. They all could have died."

A Perilous Place

Senior Lifeguard Dan Brigham described the event to our reporter.

"Apparently, the boys had been playing in the boat while it was moored, but somehow the mooring came loose and they were swept out by the tide. The children were in great danger. The sea is a perilous place, even in fine weather. The combination of a fast tide and the incoming storm meant the worst conditions possible. Thank goodness no lives were lost. It could have been a tragedy."

"So often," he commented, "we get called out because of someone's stupidity. They should never have been near the sea in these conditions."

Busiest Year Ever

The local lifeboat service has been involved in over 9,000 rescues during the year. This shows an increase of 8.5% for the area, which is higher than the national average. The service is totally manned by volunteers and relies on donations by the general public for its survival. If you would like to support their essential life-saving work, contact rnli.org.uk

KEEPING IN TOUCH

This session continues the theme of recounting events with letter writing and diary writing. Children will compare the common features and differences, and consider audience and purpose.

OBJECTIVE
To recount events in the style of a diary or letter.

WHAT YOU NEED
Photocopiable pages 43, 47, 48 and 49.

MAIN POINTS

Knowledge of purpose and audience are important when children decide on the tone and formality or informality of writing. Diaries do not usually have an audience other than the author. Exceptions are when diaries are written to be published.

DON'T PANIC!
■ Children who need extra support can make their notes on the writing frame on photocopiable page 43.
■ A letter writing frame is available to support those who need it on photocopiable page 49.

WHOLE CLASS ACTIVITY
■ Brainstorm the features and purpose of letter writing. Discuss the different purposes, for example, to recount an event, to inform, to complain, to persuade, to apologise.
■ Tell the children to focus on letters to recount events and brainstorm typical features (e.g. layout, informal greeting, informal 'chatty' tone). Draw up a list for the children's reference. Discuss the purpose of a 'recounting' letter; to inform someone else about something that happened.
■ Ask the children if any of them keep personal diaries, and why. Who do they expect to read their diaries? Brainstorm the features and purpose of diary writing. Draw up a list from the children's suggestions, for example, the audience is the writer themselves, unless a famous person expects the diary to be published, informal tone, jottings and incomplete sentences can occur, past tense verbs to recount events, date and chronological order.
■ Hand out photocopiable pages 47 and 48 to pairs of children. Ask the pairs to read the diary and the letter to each other. Ask them to suggest who they think the authors are and the intended audience is. Then tell them to identify similarities and differences. Remind them to think of Who? What? Where? When? Why? and feelings, and to mark up the extracts using coloured pens to show what the two texts have in common.
■ Gather the children together and discuss their findings. Ask the children to say what the main differences are between the two texts, for example, layout, tone, point of view, audience. Discuss how the diary entries would change if the intended audience were to change, for example, from private to public.

INDEPENDENT WRITING ACTIVITY
■ Ask the children to imagine they have been on holiday. Invite them to make notes of Who? What? When? Where and feelings. Ask them to write an imaginary diary to describe the first week of their holiday.
■ Ask them then to work with a partner and to write a letter to each other describing their holiday. Encourage them to swap letters and read their partner's. Remind the children to lay out their letters correctly, and although the tone is informal, to ensure it is legible and that the audience (their friend) will be able to understand it.

PLENARY
■ Invite children who enjoyed reading their partner's letters to read them aloud. Discuss what features made them enjoyable.
■ Ask them to say how the content of their diary entries changed when they wrote the letters, and why.

August 2006

Saturday

Arrived late Friday night. Was v tired so went straight to sleep. Explored the beach today - very quiet. Why we had to come here I don't know. Used to enjoy the busy beach and shops in Spain. Food was good tho. Met up with the others in a café in the village. Tamara looks like she'll be a pain. Wouldn't stop talking. Glad Shaz is here! We'll do our own thing.

Sunday

Bit sunburnt, but not too much.
We (Shaz and me) sunbathed most of the day. Tamara was forced on us, but we ignored her. Sea was good - big waves. Food nice again, not much else to do. Tomorrow we are all going to Sea Centre. It is miles away. Off to sleep now. Night night!

Monday

Tan getting better. Got white line where watch goes!
Sea Centre was brill. It took 2 hrs to get there but was worth it. Loads of water rides and stuff. HUGE slides. Tamara was great (surprise surprise!) We went on everything. Shaz got in a strop. She didn't like the salty water and kept saying she was too hot - the water was too cold - her head ached etc etc.
Shaz stayed in the villa tonight with her mum, so it was just Tam and me out to eat (with dreaded parents of course - apart from Shaz's mum).
Tomorrow is a day on the beach. Tam's Dad has rented a boat. It arrives in the morning. Might be fun.

Tuesday

Skin hurts a bit. Mum made me wear a T-shirt all day - with long sleeves.
Shaz didn't show up but Tamara did. Her Dad made us wear life-jackets in the boat, but it was still good.
We stayed in the villa tonight and had a BBQ, just us. Good.
Very tired so - night night!

Wednesday

Felt v bad today. Drove to Shaz's and she is ILL!!! They got a doctor who couldn't speak English so they are going home tomorrow. Poor Shaz. We made it up, and Tam gave her a bracelet.
Hope she gets better and can stay. She'll miss my birthday!!!

Writing letters

28 Millsom Terraces
Carrington
Dowchester

2nd September

Dear Isobel,

How are you? I hope the winter is being kind to you, way down there in New Zealand!

We have been away on holiday – for 3 weeks this time. We went to the Algarve, in the South of Portugal instead of Spain this time. Our friends John and Denise, and another couple called Faris and Marta joined us, with their daughters. It was such a shame for Minti – her friend Sharon became ill, so John and Denise took her home in the first week. However, Faris and Marta stayed, and Sharon became firm friends with their daughter Tamara.

We had a lovely villa near the coast, and Faris hired a boat. Imagine... me, a sailor! You might not believe it but by the end of the holiday I was really quite good at it.

The Algarve was lovely. The beaches were wide and sandy and the sea seemed much cleaner than Spain. We might go back again next year. Perhaps one day we'll be able to visit you and see NZ, but not for a year or two I suspect.

Well, I must finish now. I've got to dash to school for an Open Evening and find out what Minti will be doing. She starts at the High School soon and she is growing up so fast.

I promise to write more next time!

Love to all!

Sally
xx

www.scholastic.co.uk

Letter writing frame

Address

_____

_____

_____

_____

[for formal letter, add name and address here]

Date _____

Dear _____,

(sign off)

SCHOLASTIC
www.scholastic.co.uk

LETTERS TO COMPLAIN

OBJECTIVE
To use an appropriate tone in formal letter writing.

WHAT YOU NEED
Photocopiable pages 49, 51 and 76.

In this lesson the children explore a fictional letter written (badly) to complain. They consider audience and purpose for letter writing and layout and tone. They will examine the letter to identify what is wrong and how to improve it, and then write their own letters to complain. Demonstrating an understanding of how audience and purpose affects the tone of the letter can help them achieve higher marks in their SATs writing paper.

WHOLE CLASS ACTIVITY

■ Explain to the children that the letter they will read is from a story told entirely through letters written by a ten-year-old girl. Set the scene for them by explaining that each child in the girl's class wrote to the cast of a play after a trip to the theatre, but received only a standard reply to the whole class, rather than individual letters. Simone wrote back to complain about this.

■ Remind the children about the conventional layout, salutations and ways to sign off letters.

■ Ask the children to suggest the purpose of a letter to complain, for example, to put across a point of view, to persuade the recipient to change their mind or to put forward an opposing argument.

■ Ask the children to discuss with a partner the language features and organisation that would make a good letter to complain, then gather them together and brainstorm the features. Expect suggestions such as a formal, conventional layout, clear statements of intention and point of view, polite tone, evidence to support their points.

■ Tell them to work with their partner and read the letter on photocopiable page 51. Ask them to discuss what is good about the letter, and what is wrong with it.

■ Gather the children back together and discuss their findings. Ask the children to suggest how the letter could be improved, for example, the length, the amount of unimportant detail, the tone, the greeting, the statement of purpose. Ask the children what they think is good about the letter.

■ Collaborate with the children in re-writing the letter, using a formal greeting (Dear Jem, or Dear Mr Cakebread), stating the purpose or point of view at the beginning followed by points to support it, any opposing points, a brief summary and the correct closing phrase.

■ Encourage the children to suggest persuasive or emotive words and phrases to convince the recipient that their point is valid.

MAIN POINTS

The tone of a complaint letter should be formal and polite.
Letters to complain have the features and language conventions of persuasive text.

INDEPENDENT WRITING ACTIVITY

■ Ask the children to imagine they have all written letters to a favourite author, but only received a single impersonal reply. Tell them to write another letter to complain about it.

■ Remind the children about the purpose of the letter - to convince the recipient that their point of view is valid. What do they hope to gain by writing the letter? A more personal response?

PLENARY

■ Ask some of the children to read their letters aloud, and encourage the others to say how they would feel if they received this letter. Identify which structures and language features were the most effective.

DON'T PANIC!
■ Children who need support can use the letter frame on photocopiable page 49. The features of persuasive writing are also covered in more detail on photocopiable page 76.

Woodhill Primary School
Woodhill
Nr Bartock

July 14th

Dear Jem Cakebread alias Rumplestiltskin,

    I am writing to you in annoyance and because I have hay fever and can't do Sports Day. Miss Cassidy told me to wash the glue pots out and I've done that so now I'm writing to you.

    I'm sort of glad I'm not doing the 60 metres skipping race because Anthony Bent's in it and he always wins. I told you about him – he's the one who made me nearly die on a Tooty-frooty in the theatre but I couldn't bash him because his mum is a teacher and was sitting next to him. She said I shouldn't have been eating in the first place. She's a mardy teacher. I'll be in her class next year, worst luck.

    Miss Cassidy read your letter to us and that's why I'm writing. No offence, but I don't think it's fair that you only wrote one letter for everyone. Miss said I could have a photocopy of the letter if I was that desperate but I told her it was not the same. She said it was nice that you wrote back at all and it was hard work in the theatre but I discussed it with my mum and she said actors didn't know what hard work was. She said acting was just grown-ups playing and getting paid for it. I agree with my mum.

    Listen, it took our class three days to write our letters to you. First we had to copy down Miss's words from the board, then finish the sentences in rough then write it up in neat, then do a picture.

    It took some of my friends all week. Chloe Madelaine Shepherd had to miss two playtimes because she kept forgetting to put a 'u' in Queensgate in her best copy. Peter Bacon has special needs and rubbed holes in his letter so he had to do it on the computer in the end and that took him and his helper, Mr Cohen, ages, mainly because Mr Cohen couldn't work the computer and kept forgetting to save the text. You should always save the text, in case you didn't know. Mr Cohen is only a student. He has a ponytail. Chloe Madelaine Shepherd is in love with him but it's a secret so don't say anything.

    So my letter is a complaint letter really. My mum writes lots of complaint letters. She wrote one to our MP once she was that mad about what he said in the paper about single parents. I think that's why we don't have much money because she uses a lot of stamps.

    To summarize, therefore (my mum always writes that near the end of her letters). To summarize, therefore, I think you and the others should have written a letter back to each of us like we did to you. It is only polite. I know you would have had to write the most because you were the most popular but the Queen always writes back and she's much more popular than you, no offence. (I mean Her Royal Highness Queen Elizabeth II, not Queen Stretchy-Lycra in your play. She was stupid. Only Anthony Bent wrote to her.)

    Yours sincerely

    Simone Wibberley

    (nearly ten)

Extract from Simone's Letters by Helena Pielichaty

LESSON PLANS

MAIN POINTS

In this lesson the children review and consolidate their knowledge of the conventions used to write a non-chronological report. They make notes for writing a report of their own, and finally complete a polished version. Speedy note-making is a skill that can really help them in the SATs writing paper. Children need to be able to adjust their tone and sentence constructions to suit the required text type easily to enable them to achieve high marks.

WHOLE CLASS ACTIVITY

■ Explain to the children that they are going to write a report. Tell them that in the SATs writing paper this kind of text is often just described as an 'information text'.

■ Explain that in the test, they must ensure they write in the correct style. Explain that many non-fiction books include more than one type of text. For example, an information text may include some explanations or instructions. Emphasise how important it is to use the appropriate conventions, and in order to do this, they must think about the purpose of the text.

■ Provide the children with a selection of non-fiction books. Ask them to work with a partner and look through the books together, isolating any that they think fall into the 'report' text-type (as opposed to explanations or instructions). Divide these identified books between the pairs of children and ask them to look through them, making notes of common features of language, purpose and layout.

■ Gather the children together again to brainstorm a list of the features of reports. Write the list on the board for the children's reference. For example: a general introduction, information about a group or class of things, present tense verbs. A list of features can be found on photocopiable page 73. You may prefer to enlarge it and display it.

■ Ask the children to work with their partner and go through the text on photocopiable page 53 together, marking up any of the features from the list on the board using coloured pens.

■ Gather the children together again and ask them to explain their findings. Ask them what features were evident or missing in this text when compared to the books they explored before. They should identify that this piece contains instruction text as well. Ask what it was that signalled the change of text type. Children can compare their annotations with the annotated text on photocopiable page 55.

INDEPENDENT WRITING ACTIVITY

■ Tell the children that they are going to write a report on the subject 'Balls for sport'. Brainstorm a few examples with them - footballs, rugby balls, cricket balls, netballs, and so on.

■ Model how to make brief notes on the board using a spidergram similar to the one provided on photocopiable page 54, or enlarge a copy. Ask them to work with their partner and collaborate to make notes for their reports.

■ When they are satisfied, ask them to write their own report, using as many of the text-type conventions as are appropriate.

PLENARY

■ Ask children to read their reports aloud. Discuss the order of the information, identify good use of sub-headings and captions or labels. Discuss the benefits of sub-headings and captions or fact boxes.

Juggling balls

History

Juggling has been popular for thousands of years. Historians believe that juggling was common long before then, in Ancient Greek and Egyptian times.

In the past, jugglers were usually people who moved from town to town to earn their living. In the days before newspapers, these entertainers passed on news and gossip.

In the Middle Ages, the courts of most kings and lords had a juggler who often was also the court jester, or clown. Juggling has continued to be very popular and great jugglers of more recent times, like Enrico Rastelli, Paul Cinquevalli, Bobby May and Dick Franco have invented exciting moves, tricks and routines.

You may have seen professional jugglers juggling anything from eggs to chairs; but at the beginning, it's best to learn with ordinary juggling balls or juggling bean bags.

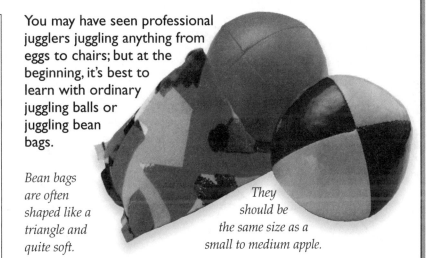

Bean bags are often shaped like a triangle and quite soft.

They should be the same size as a small to medium apple.

Size, grip, bounce and patterns

There are four things to consider when buying balls. These are their size, grip, bounce and the pattern on them. Here are the points you need to look for.

Most places will let you try holding balls.

You should just be able to hold all three balls in one hand. Two balls lying up your hand should stretch from your palm to near the top of your middle finger.

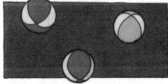

Choose bright balls that look different from each other, as they will stand out better against the background as you juggle.

You should be able to squash the balls a little.

The balls should feel comfortable to hold and not slippery. They should 'give' a little when you squeeze them. This will make them easier to control when juggling.

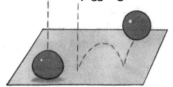

For learning to juggle, it's best to have balls which don't bounce or roll away very far when they are dropped on the floor.

Text and images © 1995, Usborne Publishing Ltd.

Report spidergram

■ Fill in the types of balls you want to write about. Add other details for each type, such as shape, size, colour, material, who plays. Add other information you think will be useful.

■ These can be used as the paragraphs for your report. It will help you organise your thoughts.

■SCHOLASTIC
www.scholastic.co.uk

LESSON PLANS
PHOTOCOPIABLE

title states what the topic is

sub heading states the aspect of the topic in the paragraph

general non-specific noun

description

generalised participants

past tense verbs used for historical information

technical terms relating to the topic

present tense verbs denote move back to current information

Present tense verbs denote move back to current information

captions

imperative verb

moves to an instruction section

Juggling balls

History
Juggling has been popular for thousands of years. Historians believe that juggling was common long before then, in Ancient Greek and Egyptian times.

In the past, jugglers were usually people who moved from town to town to earn their living. In the days before newspapers, these entertainers passed on news and gossip.

In the Middle Ages, the courts of most kings and lords had a juggler who often was also the court jester, or clown. Juggling has continued to be very popular and great jugglers of more recent times, like Enrico Rastelli, Paul Cinquevalli, Bobby May and Dick Franco have invented exciting moves, tricks and routines.

You may have seen professional jugglers juggling anything from eggs to chairs; but at the beginning, it's best to learn with ordinary juggling balls or juggling bean bags.

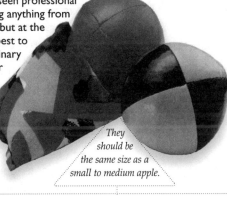

Bean bags are often shaped like a triangle and quite soft.

They should be the same size as a small to medium apple.

Size, grip, bounce and patterns
There are four things to consider when buying balls. These are their size, grip, bounce and the pattern on them. Here are the points you need to look for.

Most places will let you try holding balls.

You should be able to squash the balls a little.

You should just be able to hold all three balls in one hand. Two balls lying up your hand should stretch from your palm to near the top of your middle finger.

The balls should feel comfortable to hold and not slippery. They should 'give' a little when you squeeze them. This will make them easier to control when juggling.

Choose bright balls that look different from each other, as they will stand out better against the background as you juggle.

For learning to juggle, it's best to have balls which don't bounce or roll away very far when they are dropped on the floor.

Text and images © 1995, Usborne Publishing Ltd.

SCHOLASTIC
www.scholastic.co.uk

PLANS

OBJECTIVE
To develop a sense of audience and purpose.

WHAT YOU NEED
Photocopiable pages 57, 58, 59 and 74.

Using the conventions of different non-fiction text types in the SATs writing paper is an important factor in getting high marks. In this lesson the children identify the key elements and language structures of instruction writing. They explore two different sets of instructions, identify good or bad instructions and how they can be improved. They then write their own sets of instructions for a specific audience. Using appropriate vocabulary and tone that demonstrates a clear sense of audience and purpose will result in higher marks.

WHOLE CLASS ACTIVITY

■ With the class, review their knowledge of the conventions of instruction texts and brainstorm a list of essential features. For example: a clear opening statement of purpose, what is needed, step-by-step sequential instructions, illustrations used only when needed, imperative verbs.
■ Ask the children if other features are needed to make instructions clear to the reader. Elicit examples such as: definitions of technical or specialist terms, hazard warnings, references for further information on the topic.
■ Use Post-it Notes to cover the illustrations that accompany the instructions on photocopiable pages 57 and 58 and provide copies for pairs of children. Ask the children to work with their partner to look at both sets of instructions. Tell them to identify the key features that occur in both sets, and to find how they differ. Ask them to identify any parts that are unclear, or could benefit from added information. Ask them also to suggest who the intended audience is for each set of instructions.
■ Tell them to reveal the illustrations and discuss their importance. Invite them to discuss whether the instructions work without the illustrations.
■ Ask the children to find any sets of instructions they have written in the past.
■ Tell them to swap them with their partner and to review and improve each others' writing.
■ Ask them to report to each other on how they think they have improved each others' writing. Suggestions should include: use imperatives, provide an opening statement, use illustrations to clarify, say what is needed, and so on.

MAIN POINTS

A set of instructions should be written with the intended audience in mind. Instructions need to be organised in a logical sequential order. Sentence structures use imperative verbs.

DON'T PANIC!
■ An instructions writing frame is available on page 59 to support those who need it. The typical features of instruction text are also available on photocopiable page 74.

INDEPENDENT WRITING ACTIVITY

■ Explain that you want the children to write instructions to be read and understood by children in Year 2.
■ Brainstorm suitable topics, for example: tying shoe laces, making a pumpkin-head, making a fruit salad, and so on.
■ Ask the pairs of children to collaborate on making notes for their chosen instructions and then write up the instructions.

PLENARY

■ Ask the pairs of children to swap instructions with other pairs who have written on a different topic. Ask them to read the new sets of instructions.
■ Gather them together and discuss which instructions were clear, well set out, and easy to follow. Ask them to identify any vocabulary or structure and layout that would be difficult for their intended audience.

Making your own balls
Here's a way to make juggling balls yourself.

What you need:
3 socks (close weave, no holes); needle and thread; filling such as pearl barley or lentils (bigger things like dried peas or beans are not as good).

Use socks from different pairs for variety.

Brighten balls up by sewing on sequins.

Outdoor filling
Dried rice, lentils and beans all swell up when wet. If you plan to juggle outdoors you will need a filling that doesn't swell. You can buy bags of small, round plastic beads or pellets from most craft shops.

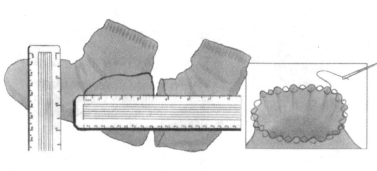
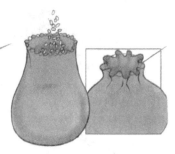

1. Measure the width of the foot of the sock. Add 1.25cm (½ inch). Measure this distance along the sock from the toe. Cut here using scissors.

2. Sew in running stitch around the top of the sock with strong thread. Leave 2.5cm (1 inch) of thread free after you've finished sewing.

3. Fill the sock with pearl barley. As it starts filling up, gently pull the thread which will draw the top of the sock together and close the hole.

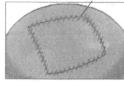

4. When the sock is almost full of pearl barley, pull the thread firmly. Keep pulling until the hole is closed as tightly as possible.

5. Cut a 4cm (1½ inch) square out of the remaining part of the sock and sew firmly over the hole. Repeat these steps to make the other two balls.

6. The balls each need to look different. Use patterned socks, or decorate them by dyeing, painting with fabric paint or sewing things on.

Text and images © 1995, Usborne Publishing Ltd.

Name _____

First faces

These instructions show you an easy way to draw cartoon faces.

Draw a circle. Do two pencil lines crossing it (1). Put the nose where the lines cross. The ears are level with the nose, and the eyes go above it (2).

When you have drawn the features, erase the pencil lines crossing the face (3). Complete the face with bright pencils or felt tips.

This shows a face seen from the front.

Looking around

As a face looks to one side, the line going down the face curves to that side.

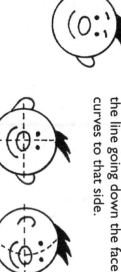

The face starts to look to one side.

The face turns even farther around.

As the face turns further around, this line also moves farther around.

A side view is called a profile.

Faces to copy

In a cartoon, you can exaggerate things such as the shape and size of the nose or mouth, to create different expressions.

Tilting heads

To make a face look up or down (1, 2 and 3) curve the line across the face up or down. To make the face look up and to one side (4) curve both lines that cross the face.

Instructions writing frame

Instructions for:
What is needed:
Numbered steps:
Outcome:
Explain any difficult vocabulary:
Write any tips or hazard warnings here:

■SCHOLASTIC
www.scholastic.co.uk

QUICK FIX FOR YEAR 6: WRITING

EXPLAIN YOURSELF

In this lesson the children explore the key features of explanation text, brainstorm connectives of cause and effect, and time, and translate an explanation diagram into written text. Demonstrating an understanding of the structure of explanation text, and a knowledge of a variety of connectives will help them raise their marks in their SATs tests.

OBJECTIVE
To focus on cause and effect language in explanation text.

WHAT YOU NEED
A selection of non-fiction books, coloured pens, photocopiable pages 61, 62, 63 and 75.

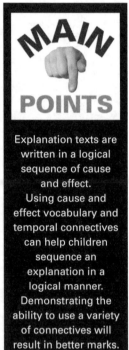

MAIN POINTS

Explanation texts are written in a logical sequence of cause and effect. Using cause and effect vocabulary and temporal connectives can help children sequence an explanation in a logical manner. Demonstrating the ability to use a variety of connectives will result in better marks.

DON'T PANIC!
■ Children who need extra support can use the writing frame on photocopiable page 63 to help them structure their explanation. The typical features of an explanation text are also available on photocopiable page 75.

WHOLE CLASS ACTIVITY
■ Provide the children with a selection of information books from the class bookshelves or the school library. Ask the children to work with a partner, flick through the books and find examples of explanation texts. Ask some of them to describe the examples they found and say why it is an explanation text (i.e. what is its primary purpose?)
■ Ask the children to give you a definition of 'explanation text'. Discuss their answers, and if no one has used the word 'cause', tell them that an explanation text tells the reader what causes something to happen.
■ Ask them, in their pairs, to discuss and draw up a list of what is needed to make a good explanation.
■ Gather the children together again and write a list of their suggested features. These should include: language of cause-and-effect, sequential information, diagrams, flow charts, labels and captions.
■ Provide them with copies of the explanation text on photocopiable page 61 and ask them to mark up any of the features they find.
■ Ask them to swap texts with their partner and compare their annotations. Did they identify the same features?

INDEPENDENT WRITING ACTIVITY
■ Provide the children with copies of photocopiable page 62. Ask the children to work with a partner and describe aloud to each other what the diagram on the page illustrates. Encourage them to use the language of cause and effect, and of time (when, if, this makes, causes, next, then, finally).
■ Ask the children to use the diagram to write an explanation, linking their points with temporal and causal connectives.

PLENARY
■ Ask the children to read their explanations to their partners without having the diagram visible. Encourage them to discuss whether the explanation makes sense, is written in a logical sequence and if they have made good use of cause and effect vocabulary. Ask them to choose the best versions to read aloud.
■ Invite them to suggest how the other versions could be improved. Discuss whether the diagram is still needed to clarify their explanations.

How a rollercoaster works

Image © Stockbyte/Punchstock

Rollercoasters are rides in fun fairs that speed along a curving track. Many people enjoy the thrill and excitement of whizzing down steep slopes, crawling slowly up hills and even turning upside down as the ride goes through loops. But have you ever wondered how a rollercoaster works?

A rollercoaster consists of a series of carriages linked together that moves along two parallel tracks, just like a train. However, unlike a train, a rollercoaster has no engine to pull or push it along. The main force involved in keeping a rollercoaster on the move is gravity.

In order to start the rollercoaster moving, a lift pulls the rollercoaster train up to the top of the first hill. This is called the lift hill. The higher the lift hill is, the greater are the forces of gravity needed to pull it down again. Once the train goes over the summit, gravity takes over and the train speeds downhill. At the next hill, the train has built up enough energy to take it up the incline. The train slows down as it climbs, as gravity is still pulling at the rear of the train. Again as it goes over the summit, the train builds up speed as gravity pulls at the front of the train.

The end of the ride

So why does a ride come to an end, if gravity keeps making it speed up and slow down?

In most rollercoaster rides, the hills and valleys decrease in size as the train moves along the ride. This is because friction between the wheels and the tracks cause the train gradually to lose momentum, so eventually it would not have sufficient energy to climb the steeper hills, and gravity would pull it backwards.

The rollercoaster ride also has brakes. This is so the train can come to a smooth stop at the end of the track. But did you know, the brakes are in the track, not on the train?

Gravity pulling down makes it speed up.

Gravity pulling down makes it slow down.

Glossary

Friction
the force that resists motion when two objects slide or roll against each other

Gravity
the force that attracts objects to the centre of the earth

Momentum
the force of motion gained by a moving object

Summit
the highest point

Name _____

How icebergs form

snow · high mountains · ice

snout · sea · iceberg

Explanation text writing frame

Title:

Opening statement:
(tell what it is)

Explanation sequence:
(tell what happens, how and why)

Result:

Closing statement:

Useful words and phrases:

nouns: snow, ice, glacier, mountain, sea, snout, iceberg, chunk
adjectives: cold, heavy, large
adverbs: slowly, gradually, heavily
connectives: at first, eventually, then, this makes,

ADVERTISING

Children are, perhaps, more familiar with how authors use inference in fictional writing than in non-fiction. They need to be shown how to include inference in their own non-fiction writing in order to improve their marks significantly. In this lesson, children explore the persuasive techniques of using rhetorical questions which imply that the author already knows the answer, and how to attract readers by understanding how layout and content can affect readers' responses.

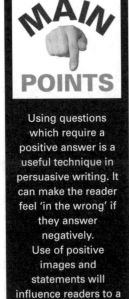

WHOLE CLASS ACTIVITY

■ Provide the pairs of children with copies of photocopiable pages 65 and 66. Ask them to work with a partner and discuss the following points: What is the purpose of each text? What do they have in common? What are their differences? How do they influence readers? Gather the children together and discuss their findings.

■ Ask the children to look at the use of punctuation in both texts. Ask them to find a punctuation mark that features in only one of the texts, such as exclamation marks in the telephone advertisement. Invite them to suggest why this text features so many exclamation marks.

■ Ask them to find where questions are used in the texts. Focus on the two questions in the telephone advertisement. Invite the children to say what answer the writer expects readers to give. Now look at the two questions at the end of 'Bats about Bats'. Can the children suggest why the author has used the phrases 'lovely jerking soundless flight', and 'summer's evening'? How does it make them feel? Ask them to suggest why the next question begins with 'wouldn't' rather than 'would'. Would they feel mean and uncaring if they answered 'no' to the question? Encourage them to think about how the two texts differ most.

■ Divide the class in half; one half to work with the advertisement for 'Bats about Bats', and the other half with the telephone advertisement. Ask them to work with a new partner, and to mark up all the features of the text that are intended to influence the reader. For example: layout, use of different font effects, italics, underlining, bold print, upper-case letters, fact and opinion.

■ Swap texts with the other half of the class and ask the children to discuss each others' findings. Are there any persuasive features they have missed?

INDEPENDENT WRITING ACTIVITY

■ Brainstorm a list of clubs or societies that the class thinks would be good for the school.

■ Ask the children to work individually to write an advertisement to persuade others to join their chosen society.

PLENARY

■ Invite several of the children to display their adverts and read them aloud to the class. Hold a vote on which society they would like to join most.

■ Discuss the reasons for their choices. Which aspects of the advertisements most influenced their choice?

Bats About Bats

For only £5 a month, **YOU** can make a difference.

The Pipistrelle Bat will survive with **YOUR** help

Under Threat

Did you know that the common Pipistrelle Bat is declining in numbers?

Causes

The overuse of insecticides combined with the destruction of hedgerows and ponds has meant that the food and habitat of the Pipistrelle bat have been greatly reduced.

When did you last see a bat's lovely, jerking soundless flight on a summer's evening?

Wouldn't you like to make a difference?

Join Bat About Bats Today

You will receive a free BAB badge and car sticker, a free bat box and instructions about how to attract bats to your garden.

Join Today!

AMAZING BAT FACTS

- The Pipistrelle bat is the smallest bat in Britain.
- It is so tiny that it can squeeze through gaps as small as 15mm wide.
- Its Latin name is Pipistrellus Pipistrellus.
- Its ancient name is Flittermouse.
- To avoid obstacles while in fast flight in the dark it uses echo-location, similar to radar.
- Bats are the only true flying mammals.

Image © Photolibrary.com

Name _____

LOOK!
The new Mobymate is here!

www.mobymate.com
The Only Phone you'll ever need!

Don't get left behind!   Keep ahead of the crowd!

Just look at all these Mobymate features!

MP3 player   **camera**   **SatNav**   **Large screen**

i-pod   **Screen-touch keying**

email   **Easy texting**

TV   **Voicemail**

internet   **Landline**

alarm clock   **DVD player**

Home-work-answer-generator
Parent/teacher-approaching alarm

It's Phonematic!!!

Want to ditch your old phone now?
Well... what's stopping you?

Only available at www.mobymate.com

See website www.mobymate.com for full details

Only £560 then **FREE** for one month

Name _____

Persuasive text writing frame

Use this frame to organise your advert. Try using different colours and sizes of writing to attract readers.

Heading and opening statement of information about your club
Ask a question
State three features about your club
State three benefits of joining
Ask a question and give an instruction

WRITING ABOUT AN ISSUE

It is quite likely that children will be asked in their SATs writing paper to express a point of view on an issue. In this lesson the children will explore the techniques used to express a strong point of view with the intention of influencing the reader. Being able to write a point of view in a logical order and pre-empt opposing points will result in higher marks.

WHOLE CLASS ACTIVITY

■ Brainstorm a list of features that occur in persuasive texts with the children. Remind them about the use of questions in persuasive writing and advertising from the previous lesson. Explain that these types of questions are known as 'loaded questions' because they encourage a certain answer.

■ Provide pairs of children with a copy of photocopiable page 69. Ask them to work with a partner to read the text together and identify its purpose. Ask them to identify any features of persuasive writing that they find in the letter.

■ Gather the children together again and go through the letter paragraph by paragraph. Point out that the opening paragraph gives a clear statement of purpose. Look at the second paragraph and ask the children if they found any emotive words (for example, overweight, problem, obesity). Ask them to read the last sentence of this paragraph. How do they think the recipient would respond to this statement? Repeat this with the third paragraph. Discuss the effect of the loaded question at the end of the paragraph.

■ Ask the children what the letter writer does in the fourth paragraph (for example, pre-empts opposition and deals with it). Point out how the letter closes with a statement of viewpoint and a call for action. Ask them to describe the tone of the letter.

■ Ask the children to look together at the letter in pairs, and mark up the layout and language (for example, new points raised in new paragraphs, connectives, varying types and lengths of sentences).

INDEPENDENT WRITING ACTIVITY

■ Discuss with the class how they travel to school each morning, and why they use their particular method of transport.

■ Suggest that the local education authority is intending to cut morning traffic in the area by making pedestrian-only access for a mile around the school.

■ Ask the children to work in small groups and brainstorm points for and against the proposal. Ask them to decide on a group viewpoint.

■ Ask them to collaborate to write a letter to the education authority stating their group's points of view on the issue.

PLENARY

■ Ask the children who were in favour of the proposal to form a group, and those against to form another group.

■ Invite the 'for' groups to read their letters aloud, then the 'against' group to read theirs.

■ Has anyone changed their minds after hearing the opposite point of view? Discuss with them which letters were most effective and why. How could the less-effective letters be improved?

Name _____

Letter to Persuade

Pollard Primary School
School Road
Pollard Rise
Netherington
Hertfordshire

15/04/07

Councillor John Smith
Netherington Education Offices
Netherington Town Hall
Netherington
Hertfordshire

Dear Sir,

We, the pupils and staff of Pollard Primary School, are writing to express our concern about the proposed closure of Netherington Town Swimming Pool.

We all read in the newspapers and hear on television that the population of this country is becoming overweight. Fast food and lack of exercise both contribute to the growing problem of obesity. In addition to this, the sale of the school playing field two years ago has meant that the only form of organised sport available to us is swimming. We are sure you agree that exercise and organised sport are important parts of children's development.

Another point we think you should bear in mind is the increasing problem of delinquency in our town centres, where children with no outlet for their energies cause trouble, mostly through sheer boredom. Netherington Pool provides much needed outlets for children's high spirits through swimming clubs and water polo. If this is no longer available, we could be seeing an increase in anti-social behaviour in our town. Surely you agree that this would be a bad thing for Netherington?

We are aware that the pool is old and costly to maintain. However we believe the effect of poor health and anti-social behaviour on the council's finances would be a far greater burden than the cost of maintaining the pool.

Don't you agree that we cannot put a price on our children's health and sense of well-being?

Netherington Pool has provided exercise and enjoyment for pupils of this school and other local schools for many years. If it closes, a valuable resource will be lost.

We believe that the council should rethink its policy on the closure of the pool, and so we urge you, as strongly as possible, to stop this.

Yours faithfully,

Alan MacDonald
For and on behalf of the staff and pupils of the school.

DISCUSS!

OBJECTIVE
To make notes in order to write a balanced discussion.

WHAT YOU NEED
Photocopiable page 71.

Discussion texts put across two or more points of view in a balanced manner to allow the reader to come to their own conclusions about an issue.
Using a variety of connectives to link opposing points will help children structure their writing in a logical manner and help them raise their marks.

DON'T PANIC!
■ Children who need extra support can use the writing frame on photocopiable page 71 to structure their discussion text.

Children might be asked to discuss two sides of an issue in their SATs writing paper. It is important that they answer the question and demonstrate an understanding of how to structure a balanced argument with effective use of connected paragraphs. In this lesson, the children discuss an issue with a partner, and collaborate to make notes of opposing viewpoints. They then write a balanced discussion individually, and write a conclusion based on evidence from their writing.

WHOLE CLASS ACTIVITY
■ Tell the class that they are going to write a balanced report, and ask them to suggest the purpose of a balanced report (for example, to put all the points for and against an issue clearly so that a reader can draw his or her own conclusions about it).
■ Brainstorm a list of issues that are relevant to the children. For example: the rights and wrongs of wearing school uniform, for and against having a school holiday, having a boys-only football team.
■ Review the children's knowledge about the language of a discussion text. If necessary, remind them that both points of view can be written in two distinct ways: as all the points for a viewpoint followed by all the points against; or 'for' and 'against' points dealt with one after another.
■ Tell the children to work with a partner and choose one issue from the list. They should then discuss the issue together, one taking a stance in favour and the other against, and make notes of all the points, balancing statement with counter-statement so that there is no bias towards a particular viewpoint.
■ Gather the children together and ask all the pairs who chose the same issue from the list to read their points, both for and against. Compile a list of the main points and key issues.
■ Discuss the layout for the report. For example, would it be more effective to take statement followed by counter-statement, or to deal with each point of view separately? Should bullet-point lists be used or complete sentences and paragraphs?
■ Brainstorm a list of connectives with the class (for example, however, therefore, nevertheless, although, and so on). Explain that these can be used to link ideas and paragraphs to make the argument flow.

INDEPENDENT WRITING ACTIVITY
■ Ask the children to write an opening paragraph to introduce the issue and then to translate their notes into a balanced report about it. Stress that the report should be balanced so they should try not to show any bias.
■ Invite the children to swap their written discussion with their partners. Encourage them to discuss what they think deserves a star and what could be improved.
■ Tell them to write a paragraph showing a conclusion for each other's balanced report.

PLENARY
■ Invite some of the children to read aloud their discussion and the conclusion added by their partner. Discuss as a class whether the concluding paragraph was what they expected as an outcome to their reports, and the effect it has on the whole piece of writing. Does the conclusion show bias?

Name _____

Discussion text writing frame

Title:
(What is the issue?)

Introduction:
(Describe the issue and why it is important)

For and against sequence:

Helpful words and phrases:
Linking statements from one point of view:
Also... In addition... Furthermore... A further point in favour of... Surveys have shown that...
Balanced statements from both points of view:
Although some people think... On the other hand... However... Nevertheless...

Summary:
(Sum up the key issues of both viewpoints)

Conclusion:
(What your partner thinks)

DON'T PANIC!

Language features and organisation of recount texts

Purpose
■ to retell events

Organisation
■ general opening statement about what is being recounted to set the scene
■ relevant information about Who? What? When? Where? Why? and How?
■ record of events in sequential order
■ concluding statement to indicate the importance or significance of the events

Language features
■ past tense verbs
■ first person and/or third person verbs
■ paragraphs used to signal a change in place, person, time or event
■ time-related connectives used to link points and events

Types of recount text
■ diary
■ biography
■ autobiography
■ newspaper reports
■ letters

Check it!
■ Are there any changes from first person to third person, or third person to first person?
■ Are paragraphs linked by different connectives? Are they used to show a change of place, time or event?
■ Make sure the verb tenses are consistent.
■ Are the sentences punctuated correctly?

SCHOLASTIC
www.scholastic.co.uk

Name _____

Language features and organisation of non-chronological reports

Purpose
■ to describe the way things are (or were historically)

Organisation
■ heading or title
■ opening statement introduces the topic
■ logical, not time-based sequence
■ describes a class of things (for example, railway trains)
■ defines the subject
■ details of facts and features about the topic
■ sometimes includes an explanation and/or instructions
■ closing statement

Language features
■ present tense verbs (unless the topic is historical when past tense verbs are used)
■ technical terms (which may need defining)
■ paragraphs used to signal changes in topic, time, or place
■ headings and subheadings
■ photographs and/or diagrams
■ captions
■ labels
■ cause and effect language

Types of non-chronological report
■ alphabetically-organised books such as an encyclopaedia or dictionary
■ general information books on the topics of nature, science, technology, sport, and so on.

Check it!
■ Have you used a clear opening statement and closing statement?
■ Is it written in the present tense?
■ Are paragraphs used to signal new facts or features?
■ Is the information ordered logically?
■ Is your punctuation correct?

■SCHOLASTIC
www.scholastic.co.uk

QUICK FIX FOR YEAR 6: WRITING

Name _____

DON'T PANIC!

Language features and organisation of instruction texts

Purpose
- to instruct how to make or do something

Organisation
- title usually states the aims or goal
- list of what is needed
- series of sequential steps
- hazard warnings and advice

Language features
- imperative verbs usually at the start of a sentence
- time-based connectives (for example, first, next, then, finally, and so on)
- numbered or bullet-pointed steps
- diagrams
- labels
- captions

Types of instruction texts
- recipes
- science experiments
- directions (how to get somewhere)
- design and technology (how to make something)
- horticulture (how to grow something)

Check it!
- Does it begin with a clear statement of the aim or what is to be achieved?
- Are all the materials listed?
- Is the order time-based?
- Have you used command verbs?
- Do the connectives make sense?

SCHOLASTIC
www.scholastic.co.uk

Language features and organisation of explanation texts

Purpose
■ to explain how or why something occurs or how something works

Organisation
■ title often uses 'how' or 'why'.
■ opening statement or paragraph tells readers what is being explained
■ described in time order and/or cause-and-effect
■ subheadings and paragraphs for shifts in place, time or event
■ can include diagrams and flow charts

Language features
■ present tense verbs (unless explaining a historical topic)
■ time-based connectives (when, next, and so on)
■ cause and effect connectives (if... then, this makes...)
■ technical and unusual vocabulary explained
■ general nouns (volcanoes, clouds, bread)

Types of explanation text
■ non-fiction books describing how or why something happens or works (What is condensation? How do volcanoes erupt?)

Check it!
■ Have you opened the explanation by telling readers what you will be explaining?
■ Is the sequence logical?
■ Have you used time-based connectives and cause and effect vocabulary?
■ Are verbs written in the present tense?
■ Have you used new paragraphs for new stages or steps in the explanation sequence?
■ Do any diagrams make something clear? Are they necessary?

www.scholastic.co.uk

QUICK FIX FOR YEAR 6: WRITING

Name _____

DON'T
PANIC!

Language features and organisation of persuasion texts

Purpose
■ to convince the reader to think or act in a particular way

Organisation
■ opening statement of position
■ series of arguments
■ supporting facts and evidence with statements of opinion
■ conclusion

Language features
■ mostly present tense verbs
■ time-based connectives
■ cause and effect connectives
■ emotive vocabulary
■ repetition to reinforce points
■ rhetorical questions
■ request for action

Types of persuasion texts
■ letters
■ leaflets
■ advertisements

Check it!
■ Have you used strong adjectives and adverbs?
■ Have you varied your use of connectives?
■ Can you use a question? Does it put an idea into your reader's mind?
■ Is your spelling and punctuation accurate?

■SCHOLASTIC
www.scholastic.co.uk

Name _____

Language features and organisation of discussion texts

Purpose
■ to describe more than two opposing points of view about an issue

Organisation
■ introduction about the issue
■ statements describing both views
■ bullet points, numbered lists
■ paragraphs
■ summary
■ conclusion

Language features
■ present tense verbs
■ connectives linking points to show connection or opposition (however, in addition to, nevertheless)
■ emotive vocabulary

Types of discussion texts
■ leaflets
■ journalism
■ advertisements

Check it!
■ Have you introduced the issue and explained why it is important?
■ Have you used a variety of connectives?
■ Have you balanced each point?
■ Does your discussion focus on the key issues involved?
■ Have you summed it up?
■ Is your punctuation correct?

www.scholastic.co.uk

QUICK FIX FOR YEAR 6: WRITING

PRACTICE PAPERS

INTRODUCING THE PRACTICE PAPERS

This lesson can be used to introduce any of the example SATs writing tasks in the section that follows. If you follow a similar format each time you work on a paper, the children will become familiar with the style of the paper and being in an exam situation. You should also remind them each time of good exam techniques.

OBJECTIVES
To become familiar with the format of the SATs writing paper tasks.
To apply good exam techniques.

WHAT YOU NEED
An example SATs writing task for each child (see photocopiable pages 80–90).

WHAT TO DO
Tell the children that during the lesson they will be given the opportunity to practise all of the writing skills and knowledge they have learned by completing a SATs writing task. They have been designed to support the children's revision by supplying them with a range of short and long writing tasks across a variety of text genre. Reassure the children and talk them through these excellent techniques for sitting exams.

■ Tell them: These are good, tried and tested exam techniques.

■ Read the tasks twice before you start to answer them – this will help you to make sure you understand the purpose of the writing task!

■ As you read the task, underline or make notes of the key words and phrases in the task.

■ Make a note of: who you are writing for (the audience); why you are writing (the purpose) and what type of writing you are being asked to do (instruction text).

■ Plan your writing before you start. Make notes of useful words and phrases. Note down ideas and then group your ideas into paragraphs. Plan how you will start and end your writing.

■ Note down any interesting words and phrases you want to use.

■ Make a note of words you can use to link your sentences and paragraphs.

■ Try to work out if the writing task is fiction or non-fiction in style, and use appropriate vocabulary and sentence structures. Even if the task asks you to use your imagination, check whether it will be a fictional piece or non-fiction.

■ Don't take too long on planning for the shorter writing task. Be precise.

■ You have ten minutes to plan your longer writing task, make use of it!

■ Your notes do not need to be neat; they are not marked.

■ Write your answer neatly – the person marking your SATs writing paper may have 300 papers to look at!

■ Take time to check your writing when it is finished. Ask yourself: Will the reader be able to understand what I have written, or will the reader be able to picture the scene in his or her head?

■ Check your punctuation. Make sure you have used capital letters and full stops to start and end sentences. Check that you have used a variety of punctuation marks.

■ Next, hand out the practice paper, read the instructions about the writing task aloud and ask the children to follow it with you. At this stage, how you use the papers is up to you. You could use exam conditions and set an appropriate time or you could let the children work through the questions informally, in pairs or teams.

MAIN POINTS

The children should use the practice papers to consolidate their previous learning –writing in response to purpose, audience and text type.

PLENARY
Choose from the following activities.

■ Work through questions and answers from the task as a whole class, or with individuals/groups.

■ Allow the children to read and mark each other's work.

■ Look for and use similar questions from past SATs writing papers.

DON'T PANIC!
■ Identify the area of difficulty and refer back to the corresponding lessons that cover these areas.

Practice paper 1

Shorter writing tasks

■ Think about your favourite place, or imagine a special place where you would like to be.

■ What do you like about it?

■ What do you see and hear there?

■ How do you feel there?

■ Your task is to describe your favourite place in order to persuade a friend to visit it with you.

■ Plan your persuasive text here and write it in full on the following page.

What I like (sights, sounds, feelings)
My special place
Why my friend would like it
My friend might object or argue that...

Practice paper 1

My special place

■ Persuade your friend to visit!

■SCHOLASTIC
www.scholastic.co.uk

Practice paper 2

■ Your school has held a jumble sale and raised enough money to buy a new school football strip or new library books.

■ Your task is to write a balanced report showing arguments for and against each one.

■ Finish your report by showing which you prefer and why.

■ Plan your balanced report here and write it in full on the following page.

Football Strip	Library books
For:	**For:**
1	1
2	2
3	3
4	4
Against:	**Against:**
1	1
2	2
3	3
4	4
Conclusion	

Practice paper 2

■ How should we spend the jumble sale money? A new football strip or new library books?

Practice paper 3

■ While you are on holiday with your family, a neighbour will be looking after your pet.

■ Write a set of instructions to tell your neighbour what to do.

■ Your pet can be real or imaginary; a cat, a dog, a hamster, a sabre-toothed tiger – anything you like.

■ Plan your instructions here and write them in full on the following page.

What is needed:
What to do:
Hazard warnings and advice:
Conclude your instructions:

83

Name _____

Practice paper 3

How to look after _____

Practice paper 4

■ An alien lands in the playground next to your classroom. No one else in your class sees it apart from you.

■ Write a description about what you saw so your friends and teacher can picture it in their minds.

■ Plan your descriptive text here and write it in full on the following page.

■ Make notes on the spidergram.

■ Add extra bubbles if you need them.

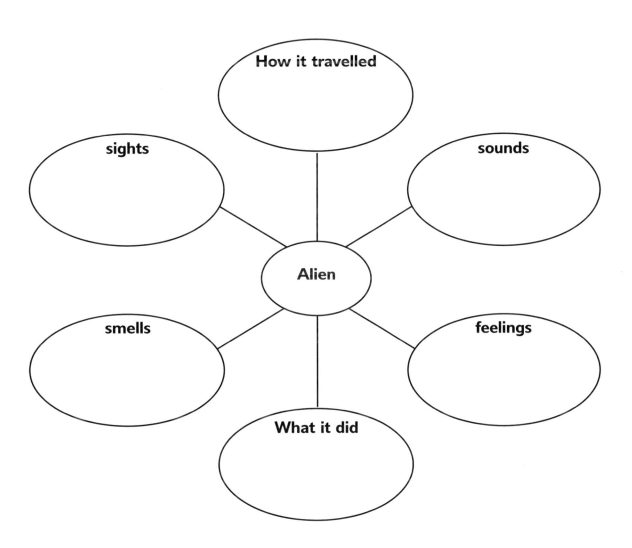

Name _____

Practice paper 4

Alien alert!

An alien landed in...

Practice paper 5

Longer writing tests

■ Your task is to write a scene for a play script about bullying.
■ There are five characters: four children and one adult.
■ Choose your own setting and the names of the characters.
■ Plan your scene using this frame and write it in full on the following page.

Child 1
Child 2
Child 3
Child 4
Adult
Who is the bully?
Who is the bully's victim?
What does the bully do?
What does the victim do?
The outcome

Name _____

Practice paper 5

The bully

SCHOLASTIC
www.scholastic.co.uk

Practice paper 6

■ Imagine your favourite author visited your school, and you were chosen to show him or her around the school.

■ Your task is to write an account of the author's visit for a school newspaper.

■ Plan your account here and write it in full on the following page.

Think about:
■ what he or she looked like
■ where you went and what you showed the author
■ what you both said
■ how you felt

Who?

Where?

What?

Linking words and phrases

QUICK FIX FOR YEAR 6: WRITING

Name _____

Practice paper 6

The day the author came to school

SCHOLASTIC
www.scholastic.co.uk

Practice paper 7

■ In an imaginary land far away, a dragon is terrorising a village. The villagers decide to seek for a hero to defeat the dragon and save the village.

■ Your task is to describe how the villagers find their hero, and how he defeats the dragon.

■ Use the organiser to plan your story and then write it in full on the following page.

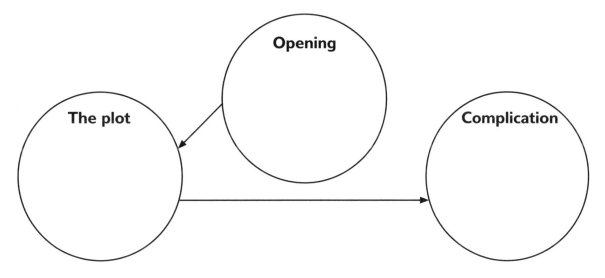

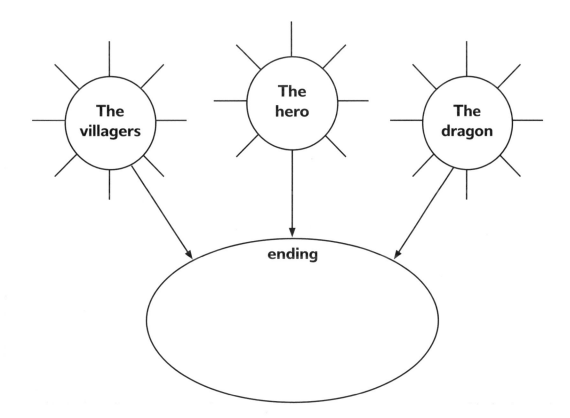

Name _____

Practice paper 7

The dragon's defeat

Practice paper 8

The life cycle of a dragonfly
■ Look carefully at the diagram of a dragonfly's life cycle.
■ Use the frame to plan your explanation of the life cycle and write it in full on the following page.

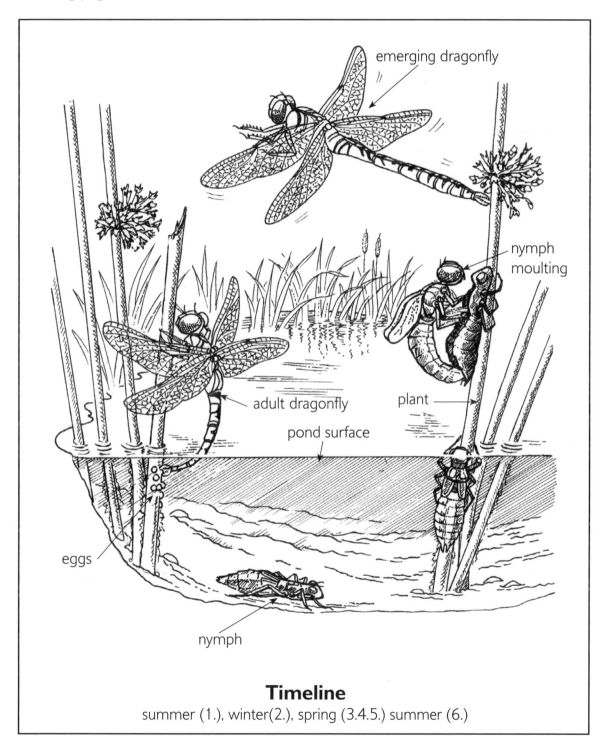

Timeline
summer (1.), winter(2.), spring (3.4.5.) summer (6.)

Practice paper 8

Title:

Opening statement:
(tell what it is)

Explanation sequence:
(tell what happens, how and why)

Result:

Closing statement:

Useful words and phrases:

nouns:

adjectives:

adverbs:

connectives:

Practice paper 8

The life cycle of a dragonfly